Discover ... ild Confidence, Belief, and ... ative Guide to Personal Growth

Unleashing Your Inner Power

Discover the Keys to Self-empowerment, Build Confidence, Belief, and Self-esteem with this Transformative Guide to Personal Growth

N. K. Daniel

The Readers Paradise
New Delhi - 110002

Unleashing Your Inner Power

N. K. Daniel

ISBN - 978-93-5977-684-2

Published by The Readers Paradise
www.thereadersparadise.com

Printed and bound by CPI Group (UK) Ltd, Croydon, CR0 4YY

Cover Design by Kamini Bijoria

Typeset by The Readers Paradise

First Edition: 2024

MIX
Paper | Supporting responsible forestry
FSC® C171272

Contents

1

Understanding Confidence, Belief and Self-Esteem

In today's fast-paced and demanding world, confidence, belief, and self-esteem play crucial roles in shaping our lives. They influence our decisions, actions, and overall well-being. Understanding the nature and dynamics of these traits is the first step toward unlocking our true potential and living a fulfilling life. Confidence, belief, and self-esteem are closely related psychological concepts that influence our thoughts, emotions, and behaviors.

Defining Confidence, Belief, and Self-Esteem:

Confidence: Confidence refers to a belief in one's abilities, skills, and judgment. It is the belief that you have the capability to accomplish a particular task or handle a situation effectively. Confidence is often built through experience, competence, and positive reinforcement. It involves a sense of self-assurance and a willingness to take risks. Confidence can vary in different areas of life, such as academic performance, social interactions, or professional pursuits. Confidence is the belief in one's abilities, competence, and worth. It involves trusting oneself to handle challenges, make decisions, and pursue goals with a sense of assurance. Confidence allows us to step outside our comfort zones, take risks, and embrace new opportunities.

Belief: Belief is a mental acceptance or conviction that something is true or exists. It is an acceptance of a proposition or statement without requiring empirical evidence. Beliefs can be formed through personal experiences, upbringing, cultural influences, and exposure to information. Beliefs can be rational or irrational, and they significantly impact our perceptions, attitudes, and behaviors. They may influence how confident we feel about certain aspects of life. Belief refers to our deeply held convictions and perspectives about ourselves, others, and the world around us. It encompasses our thoughts, values, and expectations. Our beliefs shape our self-perception, influencing our level of confidence and the actions we take.

Self-Esteem: Self-esteem refers to the overall subjective evaluation of one's worth, value, and competence as an individual. It reflects an individual's self-perception and self-worth. High self-esteem involves having a positive view of oneself, recognizing one's strengths, and believing in one's abilities. On the other hand, low self-esteem is characterized by negative self-perception, self-doubt, and a diminished sense of self-worth. Self-esteem can be influenced by various factors, including personal achievements, social relationships, body image, and internal self-talk. Self-esteem is the overall assessment of our worth and value as individuals. It reflects how we perceive ourselves and the level of self-acceptance we have. High self-esteem is characterized by a positive self-image, self-respect, and a healthy sense of self-worth.

While these concepts are distinct, they can influence and interact with one another. For example, having confidence in a particular skill or ability can contribute to higher self-esteem, as success and competence in that area can boost one's overall sense of worth. Similarly, positive beliefs about oneself can enhance confidence and reinforce a healthy self-esteem. Conversely, low self-esteem or negative beliefs can erode confidence and hinder one's ability to engage in certain activities or take risks.

It's important to note that confidence, belief, and self-esteem are subjective experiences that can vary from person to person and across different situations. Developing and maintaining healthy levels of confidence, belief, and self-esteem often involves self-reflection, challenging negative beliefs, building on strengths, seeking support when needed, and engaging in activities that promote personal growth and achievement.

The Interconnectedness of Confidence, Belief, and Self-Esteem

Confidence, belief, and self-esteem are interconnected and can influence one another in various ways. Here are some key aspects of their interconnectedness:

1. Self-perception: Self-esteem plays a significant role in shaping our overall self-perception. If someone has high self-esteem, they are more likely to have a positive view of themselves, which can contribute to a greater sense of confidence in their abilities. Conversely, individuals with low self-esteem may struggle to believe in themselves or have confidence in their capabilities.

2. Beliefs and self-efficacy: Beliefs about one's abilities, skills, and potential can have a direct impact on confidence levels. Positive beliefs in one's competence increase confidence, making individuals more willing to take on challenges and pursue their goals. On the other hand, negative beliefs or doubts about one's abilities can undermine confidence and lead to self-doubt.

3. Feedback and reinforcement: Feedback and external validation can significantly influence confidence and self-esteem. Positive feedback and recognition for accomplishments can boost confidence and reinforce positive beliefs about oneself, thereby contributing to a healthier self-esteem. Conversely, frequent negative feedback or criticism can erode confidence and self-esteem, leading to self-doubt and diminished beliefs in one's abilities.

4. Achievement and competence: Confidence and self-esteem are closely tied to one's achievements and sense of competence. Accomplishing goals and experiencing

success can enhance confidence and reinforce positive beliefs about one's abilities, leading to higher self-esteem. Conversely, repeated failures or setbacks can challenge confidence, impact beliefs, and negatively affect self-esteem.

5. Self-talk and Mind-set: The internal dialogue and self-talk we engage in can significantly impact confidence, belief, and self-esteem. Positive and supportive self-talk can foster confidence and reinforce positive beliefs about oneself. Conversely, negative self-talk or a fixed Mind-set can undermine confidence and reinforce self-doubt, limiting belief in one's capabilities and impacting self-esteem.
6. Social factors: Social interactions, relationships, and societal influences can shape confidence, beliefs, and self-esteem. Supportive and nurturing environments that encourage personal growth and self-acceptance can foster confidence and positive beliefs. Conversely, negative social interactions, criticism, or societal pressures can contribute to lower confidence and self-esteem.

It's important to note that the interconnectedness of these concepts means that working on improving one aspect can have positive ripple effects on the others. For example, building confidence through skill development and positive self-talk can gradually improve self-esteem and enhance positive beliefs about oneself. Similarly, cultivating more positive beliefs can contribute to increased confidence and healthier self-esteem.

Taking a holistic approach to developing confidence, belief, and self-esteem involves addressing underlying factors, challenging negative beliefs, building on strengths, seeking support when needed, and engaging in activities that promote personal growth and achievement.

Confidence, belief, and self-esteem are interwoven and mutually reinforcing. They form a dynamic system where each element impacts the others. A strong belief system can enhance confidence, while low self-esteem can hinder belief and confidence. Nurturing these traits collectively contributes to personal growth, resilience, and the ability to navigate life's challenges.

The Importance of Cultivating Confidence, Belief, and Self-Esteem:

1. Empowerment and Personal Growth: Confidence, belief, and self-esteem empower individuals to pursue their passions, overcome obstacles, and achieve their goals. They provide the necessary foundation for personal growth and development.
2. Resilience and Adaptability: High levels of confidence, belief, and self-esteem contribute to resilience, enabling individuals to bounce back from setbacks, embrace change, and adapt to new circumstances.
3. Positive Relationships: Cultivating confidence, belief, and self-esteem enhances interpersonal relationships. When we have a positive self-perception, we attract healthier connections and build more fulfilling connections with others.
4. Mental and Emotional Well-being: Confidence, belief, and self-esteem have a profound impact on mental and emotional well-being. They reduce stress, anxiety, and depression, promoting overall psychological health.
5. Professional Success: Confidence, belief, and self-esteem are critical in professional settings. They influence career choices, job performance, and leadership abilities, leading to greater success and satisfaction.

By delving into the depths of confidence, belief, and self-esteem, we embark on a transformative journey toward self-discovery and self-empowerment. In the following chapters, we will explore practical strategies and techniques for building and nurturing these essential traits, enabling us to unlock our true potential and live a life of confidence, belief, and self-esteem.

Confidence, belief, and self-esteem are interconnected and mutually influential. They form a dynamic system that shapes our thoughts, emotions, and behaviors. Understanding their interconnectedness is key to cultivating a healthy and empowering Mind-set. Let's explore how these traits interact:

1. Confidence and Belief: Confidence is closely tied to belief. Our beliefs about ourselves, our abilities, and the world around us greatly influence our level of confidence. When we hold empowering beliefs, such as "I am capable" or "I can learn and grow," our confidence naturally increases. Conversely, limiting beliefs, such as "I'm not good enough" or "I will fail," can erode confidence. By examining and reshaping our beliefs, we can enhance our confidence and embrace new challenges with a positive Mind-set.
2. Belief and Self-Esteem: Our self-esteem is deeply influenced by our beliefs. The beliefs we hold about our worth, capabilities, and inherent value shape our self-perception and self-acceptance. When we hold positive beliefs about ourselves, such as "I am deserving of love and respect" or "I have unique strengths," our self-esteem is bolstered. On the other hand, negative beliefs, such as "I am unworthy" or "I am a failure," can erode our self-esteem. By cultivating empowering beliefs and challenging negative self-perceptions, we can nurture a healthy and positive sense of self-worth.
3. Self-Esteem and Confidence: Self-esteem and confidence are intricately linked. When we have a healthy level of self-esteem, we tend to exhibit higher levels of confidence. Believing in our inherent worth and value provides a solid foundation for self-assurance. On the other hand, low self-esteem can undermine confidence, leading to self-doubt and a fear of taking risks. By working on building our self-esteem through self-

compassion, self-acceptance, and embracing our strengths, we can cultivate the confidence needed to pursue our goals and aspirations.

It is important to recognize that the interconnectedness of confidence, belief, and self-esteem is dynamic and ever-evolving. As we consciously work on strengthening these traits, they reinforce one another, creating a positive feedback loop. Building confidence enhances our beliefs, which in turn strengthens self-esteem. Likewise, nurturing self-esteem leads to increased confidence and the ability to embrace empowering beliefs.

By acknowledging and actively nurturing these interconnected traits, we can create a powerful foundation for personal growth, resilience, and a more fulfilling life. Through self-reflection, Mind-set shifts, and intentional practices, we can cultivate a harmonious relationship between confidence, belief, and self-esteem, unlocking our true potential and living with authenticity and self-assurance.

The Importance of Cultivating these Traits in Various Aspects of Life

Cultivating confidence, belief, and self-esteem is important across various aspects of life because they significantly influence our thoughts, emotions, behaviors, and overall well-being. Here are some key reasons why these traits are important in different areas:

1. Personal Development and Growth: Confidence, belief, and self-esteem are essential for personal growth and development. They provide the motivation and drive to set and pursue meaningful goals, overcome challenges, and explore new opportunities. Cultivating these traits enables individuals to learn and acquire new skills, expand their knowledge, and achieve their full potential. Cultivating confidence, belief, and self-esteem is fundamental to personal growth. When we have

confidence in ourselves and our abilities, we are more likely to set and achieve meaningful goals. Believing in our potential and embracing a growth Mind-set fuels our motivation to learn, develop new skills, and expand our horizons. Self-esteem provides the foundation for self-acceptance, resilience, and the willingness to take risks. By nurturing these traits, we create an environment conducive to continuous self-improvement and personal transformation.

2. Relationships and Social Interactions: Confidence, belief, and self-esteem play a crucial role in establishing and maintaining healthy relationships. When individuals have a positive self-perception and believe in their own worth, they are more likely to engage in positive and authentic interactions with others. Healthy self-esteem fosters assertiveness, effective communication, and the ability to set boundaries, which contributes to building strong and fulfilling relationships. Confidence, belief, and self-esteem significantly impact our relationships with others. When we have a healthy sense of self-worth, we enter into relationships from a place of authenticity and self-assuredness. This enables us to form healthier connections, set boundaries, and express our needs and desires. Confidence allows us to communicate effectively, assert ourselves, and build trust with others. Believing in ourselves and our worthiness of love and respect promotes fulfilling and balanced relationships.

3. Academic and Professional Success: Confidence, belief, and self-esteem are vital for success in academic and professional settings. Believing in one's abilities and having confidence in one's knowledge and skills promotes a proactive approach to learning and professional development. These traits facilitate effective problem-solving, decision-making, and resilience in the face of challenges, ultimately leading

to improved academic and career outcomes. Confidence, belief, and self-esteem play a vital role in professional success. Confidence empowers us to take on new challenges, seek growth opportunities, and showcase our skills and expertise. Believing in our abilities and maintaining a positive Mind-set fuels our motivation and perseverance in the face of obstacles. Self-esteem influences how we present ourselves in the workplace, our ability to handle criticism, and our willingness to take on leadership roles. Cultivating these traits enhances job performance, facilitates career advancement, and fosters a positive work environment.

4. Mental and Emotional Well-being: Cultivating confidence, belief, and self-esteem is crucial for overall mental and emotional well-being. When individuals have a positive self-perception and believe in their abilities, they are more likely to experience lower levels of stress, anxiety, and depression. High self-esteem provides a buffer against negative self-talk, self-doubt, and harsh self-criticism, contributing to a more positive and resilient Mind-set. Cultivating confidence, belief, and self-esteem contributes to overall emotional well-being. When we have a positive self-perception and belief in ourselves, we experience greater self-acceptance, self-compassion, and emotional resilience. Confidence allows us to manage stress, overcome challenges, and maintain a positive outlook. Belief in our own worthiness and capabilities promotes a sense of inner peace and contentment. Nurturing these traits enhances emotional stability, reduces anxiety and depression, and fosters a greater sense of fulfillment in life.

5. Decision-making and Risk-taking: Confidence, belief, and self-esteem enable individuals to step out of their comfort zones, take calculated risks, and seize opportunities for personal and professional growth.

These traits provide the courage and belief in oneself necessary to face uncertainty and embrace new challenges. Without confidence and belief in their abilities, individuals may shy away from opportunities, hindering their personal and professional development. Confidence, belief, and self-esteem are essential for making effective decisions and taking calculated risks. When we have confidence in our judgment and trust in our abilities, we are more likely to make decisions aligned with our values and goals. Belief in ourselves allows us to step out of our comfort zones, embrace uncertainty, and take risks necessary for growth and progress. By cultivating these traits, we become more resilient in the face of failure, bounce back from setbacks, and learn from our experiences.

6. Resilience and coping with setbacks: Confidence, belief, and self-esteem contribute to resilience and the ability to bounce back from setbacks and failures. When individuals have a healthy self-perception and confidence in their abilities, they are more likely to view setbacks as learning experiences, maintain a positive outlook, and persist in the face of adversity. These traits enhance emotional resilience and help individuals navigate difficult situations with greater ease.

Cultivating confidence, belief, and self-esteem in various aspects of life promotes personal growth, positive relationships, achievement, well-being, and resilience. By developing and nurturing these traits, individuals can lead more fulfilling lives and effectively navigate the challenges and opportunities that arise in different areas of life.

In all aspects of life, cultivating confidence, belief, and self-esteem empowers us to live authentically, embrace challenges, and pursue our aspirations. These traits act as catalysts for personal fulfilment, meaningful relationships, and professional success. By actively nurturing and developing these traits, we lay a solid foundation for a balanced and thriving life.

2

Self-Awareness: The Key to Unleashing Your Potential

Self-awareness is the cornerstone of personal growth and unleashing one's true potential. It is the ability to objectively observe and understand oneself, including thoughts, emotions, behaviors, and patterns. By cultivating self-awareness, we gain valuable insights into our strengths, weaknesses, values, and aspirations, empowering us to make intentional choices and live a more fulfilling life.

Self-awareness refers to the conscious knowledge and understanding of oneself, including one's thoughts, emotions, strengths, weaknesses, values, and beliefs. It involves being in tune with one's internal experiences and having an objective perception of oneself. Self-awareness is a fundamental aspect of personal growth, introspection, and understanding one's own behavior and impact on others.

Here are some key points about self-awareness:

1. Internal reflection: Self-awareness involves regularly engaging in introspection and self-reflection to gain insight into one's thoughts, emotions, and motivations. It requires taking the time to examine one's beliefs, values, and behaviors, and understanding how they shape one's actions and interactions with others.

2. Emotional intelligence: Self-awareness is closely tied to emotional intelligence, which involves recognizing and understanding one's own emotions as well as the emotions of others. By being aware of one's emotional

state, individuals can better manage their emotions, regulate their reactions, and empathize with others.

3. Recognizing strengths and weaknesses: Self-awareness helps individuals identify their strengths, talents, and areas for growth. It allows for a realistic assessment of one's abilities and limitations, which can guide personal and professional development efforts.
4. Improved decision-making: Self-awareness contributes to better decision-making by helping individuals align their choices with their values, goals, and personal fulfillment. Being aware of one's values and priorities enables individuals to make choices that are in line with their authentic selves and long-term well-being.
5. Enhanced interpersonal relationships: Self-awareness positively impacts relationships with others. When individuals have a deep understanding of their own emotions, triggers, and communication styles, they can better navigate conflicts, manage relationships, and effectively express themselves. Additionally, self-awareness fosters empathy and understanding toward others' perspectives and experiences.
6. Personal growth and self-acceptance: Self-awareness is a catalyst for personal growth and self-acceptance. It allows individuals to identify areas for improvement, set realistic goals, and develop strategies for personal development. Furthermore, self-awareness helps individuals embrace their strengths and weaknesses, leading to increased self-acceptance and self-esteem.
7. Authenticity and congruence: Self-awareness supports living an authentic and congruent life. When individuals have a clear understanding of their values, beliefs, and desires, they can align their actions and behaviors with their true selves. This alignment enhances a sense of authenticity, fulfillment, and overall well-being.

Developing self-awareness involves various practices such as mindfulness, journaling, seeking feedback from others, engaging in introspective exercises, and practicing active self-reflection. It is an ongoing process that requires openness, curiosity, and a willingness to explore and understand oneself at deeper levels. By cultivating self-awareness, individuals can make more intentional choices, build healthier relationships, and live more fulfilling lives.

The Power of Self-Awareness

The power of self-awareness lies in its ability to transform and empower individuals in various aspects of their lives. Here are some ways in which self-awareness can have a profound impact:

1. Personal growth and development: Self-awareness is a key driver of personal growth. By understanding oneself at a deeper level, individuals can identify patterns, habits, and behaviors that may be hindering their progress. Self-awareness allows for introspection and recognition of areas for improvement, leading to personal development and the acquisition of new skills and qualities.

2. Improved decision-making: Self-awareness enhances decision-making by providing individuals with a clear understanding of their values, goals, and priorities. It helps in aligning decisions with personal values and long-term aspirations, leading to more thoughtful and informed choices. Self-awareness also enables individuals to consider their emotions, biases, and intuitive insights when making decisions, resulting in more authentic and fulfilling outcomes.

3. Building authentic relationships: Self-awareness plays a crucial role in forming and nurturing healthy and meaningful relationships. By understanding one's own emotions, triggers, and communication styles,

individuals can better navigate interactions with others. Self-awareness fosters empathy, emotional intelligence, and the ability to understand and respond to others' needs and perspectives, leading to stronger and more authentic connections.

4. Emotional regulation and resilience: Self-awareness allows individuals to recognize and understand their own emotions, including their triggers and patterns. This awareness provides the foundation for emotional regulation, enabling individuals to manage their emotions effectively, make sound decisions even under pressure, and navigate challenging situations with resilience. Self-awareness helps individuals respond to emotions rather than react impulsively, leading to healthier emotional well-being.

5. Increased self-acceptance and self-esteem: Self-awareness promotes self-acceptance by acknowledging one's strengths, weaknesses, and limitations. It allows individuals to embrace their authentic selves and cultivate a positive self-image. Through self-awareness, individuals can identify and challenge negative self-talk, self-doubt, and self-limiting beliefs, leading to increased self-esteem and self-confidence.

6. Effective leadership: Self-awareness is a critical trait for effective leadership. Leaders who are self-aware understand their own strengths, weaknesses, and leadership style, which allow them to lead authentically and inspire others. Self-aware leaders are more open to feedback, able to adapt their behaviors, and make decisions that align with their values and the needs of their team or organization.

7. Personal well-being and fulfilment: Self-awareness contributes to overall well-being and fulfilment. By understanding one's own needs, desires, and sources of joy, individuals can make choices that prioritize their

well-being. Self-awareness enables individuals to create a life that aligns with their values, passions, and purpose, leading to a greater sense of fulfilment and satisfaction.

8. Recognizing Strengths and Weaknesses: Self-awareness allows us to identify and embrace our unique strengths. By understanding our capabilities, talents, and passions, we can focus on areas where we excel and maximize our potential. Similarly, self-awareness helps us recognize our weaknesses and areas for improvement, enabling us to take proactive steps toward growth and development.

9. Understanding Emotions and Reactions: Self-awareness involves tuning into our emotions and understanding how they impact our thoughts and behaviors. By developing emotional intelligence, we can better manage our emotions, respond to challenges effectively, and build healthier relationships. Understanding our triggers, stressors, and emotional patterns empowers us to make conscious choices rather than being driven by unconscious reactions.

10. Aligning with Values and Aspirations: Self-awareness enables us to clarify our values, beliefs, and aspirations. When we are in tune with our core values, we can make choices that align with our authentic selves, leading to a greater sense of fulfillment and purpose. By exploring our aspirations and understanding what truly matters to us, we can set meaningful goals and pursue paths that resonate with our deepest desires.

11. Uncovering Limiting Beliefs and Patterns: Self-awareness helps us uncover limiting beliefs, self-sabotaging patterns, and negative self-talk that hold us back. By shining a light on these internal barriers, we can challenge and reframe them, cultivating empowering beliefs that support our growth and

success. Self-awareness also allows us to identify recurring patterns in our lives, both positive and negative, and make conscious choices to reinforce or break them.

Cultivating Self-Awareness

Self-awareness is a journey that involves different aspects of life, including feelings, behaviors, and thoughts. It centres on introspection. This psychological state will force you to focus on yourself as an individual with a personality. That's why you'll find that some people are confident, always humble, and full of wisdom while remaining true to their beliefs.

Cultivating self-awareness is an ongoing process that requires intentional effort and practice. Here are some strategies that can help in developing self-awareness:

1. Practice mindfulness: Mindfulness involves being fully present in the moment and observing your thoughts, emotions, and sensations without judgment. Regular mindfulness meditation or other mindfulness practices can help you develop the ability to observe your inner experiences objectively and increase self-awareness. Mindfulness, such as meditation, breathing exercises, and present-moment awareness, enhances self-awareness by fostering non-judgmental observation of our thoughts, emotions, and bodily sensations. Regular mindfulness practices help us develop a deeper understanding of ourselves and cultivate a sense of presence and clarity.

2. Engage in self-reflection: Set aside dedicated time for self-reflection. Journaling, introspective exercises, or simply taking quiet moments to reflect on your thoughts, feelings, and experiences can help you gain insights into your patterns, values, and motivations.

3. Seek feedback: Actively seek feedback from others, such as trusted friends, family members, mentors, or

colleagues. Listen openly to their perspectives, insights, and observations about your behavior, strengths, and areas for improvement. This external feedback can provide valuable insights and different perspectives on your self-awareness journey.

4. Explore your values and beliefs: Take time to identify and clarify your personal values and beliefs. Reflect on what is important to you and what principles guide your actions. Understanding your values can help you make choices and decisions that align with your authentic self.

5. Practice self-observation: Throughout your daily life, pay attention to your thoughts, emotions, and reactions in various situations. Observe how you respond to different triggers or challenges. Notice any patterns or recurring themes in your behavior. This self-observation can help you uncover underlying beliefs, habits, or emotions that may influence your actions.

6. Seek different perspectives: Engage in conversations with people who have diverse perspectives and backgrounds. Listen to their viewpoints, challenge your own assumptions, and consider alternative ways of thinking. This exposure to different perspectives can broaden your understanding of yourself and the world around you.

7. Embrace discomfort and reflect on failures: Growth and self-awareness often come from moments of discomfort and failure. Embrace these experiences as opportunities for learning and reflection. Reflect on what led to the situation, your role in it, and how you can grow and improve from it. This introspection can lead to valuable insights and increased self-awareness.

8. Practice self-compassion: Be kind and compassionate toward yourself throughout your self-awareness journey. Acknowledge that self-awareness is a process,

and it's normal to have areas of growth and improvement. Treat yourself with patience, understanding, and self-acceptance as you explore and deepen your self-awareness.

9. Reflection and Journaling: Taking time for reflection and journaling allows us to explore our thoughts, feelings, and experiences in a structured way. Writing down our reflections helps us gain insights, identify patterns, and track our progress over time. Journaling prompts can guide us in exploring specific aspects of ourselves and our lives.
10. Seeking Feedback and Support: Engaging in open and honest conversations with trusted friends, mentors, or therapists can provide valuable external perspectives and insights. Seeking constructive feedback helps us gain a more comprehensive understanding of ourselves and areas for growth. It is important to approach feedback with an open mind and a willingness to learn and improve.
11. Continuous Learning and Self-Exploration: Engaging in continuous learning, reading books, attending workshops, and exploring new areas of interest broadens our horizons and deepens our self-awareness. Embracing curiosity and a growth Mind-set allows us to expand our understanding of ourselves and the world around us.

Remember, developing self-awareness takes time and consistent effort. Embrace it as an ongoing journey of self-discovery and personal growth.

Self-awareness is a powerful tool for personal transformation and unleashing our full potential. By cultivating self-awareness, we gain a deeper understanding of ourselves, our emotions, and our behaviors. We become better equipped to make conscious choices, align with our values, and navigate life's challenges with authenticity and purpose. Through self-reflection, mindfulness, and seeking external perspectives, we embark on

Exploring the Power of Self-awareness

Self-awareness is a transformative and empowering quality that allows us to understand ourselves on a deeper level. By exploring and harnessing the power of self-awareness, we can unlock hidden potentials, make conscious choices, and create a life aligned with our true selves. The power of self-awareness is profound and can positively impact various aspects of your life. Here are some ways in which self-awareness can be powerful:

1. Personal growth and development: Self-awareness is a catalyst for personal growth. By understanding your thoughts, emotions, strengths, and weaknesses, you can make conscious choices to improve yourself. It enables you to identify areas for development, set meaningful goals, and take intentional actions to enhance your skills, knowledge, and overall well-being.
2. Authenticity and self-acceptance: Self-awareness allows you to embrace your true self and live authentically. When you are aware of your values, beliefs, and desires, you can align your actions and choices with your authentic self. This alignment promotes self-acceptance, reduces the need for external validation, and fosters a sense of inner fulfillment and contentment.
3. Improved relationships: Self-awareness enhances your interpersonal relationships. By understanding your own emotions, triggers, and communication patterns, you can navigate conflicts, express your needs effectively, and empathize with others. It enables you to develop stronger connections, build trust, and establish healthier boundaries in your relationships.

4. Emotional intelligence: Self-awareness is a cornerstone of emotional intelligence. When you are self-aware, you can recognize and understand your emotions, which enables you to regulate them effectively. This skill helps you respond to challenges and stressful situations with greater emotional resilience and empathy towards others.
5. Effective decision-making: Self-awareness empowers you to make decisions aligned with your values, goals, and aspirations. By understanding your own biases, motivations, and thought patterns, you can make more informed and thoughtful choices. Self-awareness also helps you assess potential outcomes, consider different perspectives, and evaluate the impact of your decisions on yourself and others.
6. Leadership effectiveness: Self-awareness is a key trait of successful leaders. When leaders are self-aware, they can understand their strengths, limitations, and leadership styles. This understanding enables them to lead with authenticity, adapt their approach to different situations, and build strong, cohesive teams. Self-aware leaders are more attuned to the needs of their team members and can provide effective guidance and support.
7. Resilience and stress management: Self-awareness helps you recognize the signs of stress, burnout, and emotional exhaustion. By understanding your own limits and triggers, you can take proactive steps to manage stress effectively. Self-awareness also allows you to identify and challenge negative thought patterns, cultivate a positive Mind-set, and develop coping strategies to navigate challenging situations with resilience.
8. Life satisfaction and well-being: Self-awareness contributes to overall life satisfaction and well-being.

When you are self-aware, you can align your life choices, activities, and relationships with what brings you joy, meaning, and fulfillment. This alignment promotes a sense of purpose, reduces internal conflicts, and enhances overall happiness and well-being.

9. Understanding Thoughts and Emotions: Self-awareness begins with recognizing and understanding our thoughts and emotions. It involves observing our mental processes and becoming aware of the patterns, biases, and narratives that shape our inner world. By developing this level of self-awareness, we can gain control over our thoughts, challenge negative thinking patterns, and cultivate a more positive and balanced Mind-set.

10. Enhancing Emotional Intelligence: Emotional intelligence is closely linked to self-awareness. It involves recognizing and managing our own emotions as well as understanding and empathizing with the emotions of others. By becoming self-aware of our emotional states, we can regulate our responses, communicate effectively, and build stronger and more fulfilling relationships. Emotional intelligence allows us to navigate conflicts, resolve issues, and create a supportive and harmonious environment.

11. Uncovering Core Values and Beliefs: Self-awareness helps us uncover our core values and beliefs, which are the guiding principles that shape our lives. By exploring and clarifying our values, we can make choices that align with our authentic selves and lead to a greater sense of purpose and fulfillment. Understanding our beliefs allows us to challenge any limiting or negative beliefs that may be holding us back and replace them with empowering and supportive ones.

12. Identifying Strengths and Areas for Growth: Self-awareness enables us to identify and leverage our

strengths. By recognizing our unique talents, skills, and abilities, we can focus our energy and efforts on activities that bring out the best in us. Additionally, self-awareness helps us identify areas for growth and development. It allows us to acknowledge our weaknesses or areas where we may need improvement and take proactive steps to enhance those aspects of ourselves.

13. Making Conscious Choices: Self-awareness empowers us to make conscious choices rather than operating on autopilot. By being aware of our thoughts, emotions, and values, we can make decisions that are aligned with our authentic selves and long-term goals. This level of self-awareness helps us avoid impulsive or reactive behavior and make choices that lead to personal growth, success, and overall well-being.
14. Fostering Personal Growth and Resilience: Self-awareness is the foundation for personal growth and resilience. By understanding ourselves deeply, we can recognize our triggers, patterns of behavior, and areas where we may be holding ourselves back. This awareness allows us to break free from self-imposed limitations, embrace challenges, and learn from our experiences. It fosters a Mind-set of continuous growth and empowers us to navigate life's ups and downs with resilience and adaptability.

Cultivating self-awareness is a lifelong journey that involves self-reflection, introspection, mindfulness, and seeking feedback from others. Embracing the power of self-awareness allows you to live a more authentic, fulfilling, and empowered life.

The power of self-awareness lies in its ability to illuminate our inner world, leading to personal growth, authentic living, and enhanced well-being. By understanding our thoughts, emotions, values, strengths, and areas for growth, we gain control over our lives and can make choices that align with our true selves. Through self-reflection, mindfulness practices, and a commitment to continuous learning, we can explore the depths of self-awareness and embark on a transformative journey of self-discovery and personal empowerment.

Recognizing and Embracing Your Strengths and Weaknesses

Recognizing and embracing both our strengths and weaknesses is a vital aspect of personal growth and self-awareness. By understanding and appreciating our unique qualities and areas for improvement, we can leverage our strengths to achieve success while actively working on our weaknesses to unlock our full potential. Recognizing our strengths allows us to tap into our inherent abilities and talents. When we acknowledge what we excel at, we can leverage those strengths to enhance our performance, increase our self-confidence, and pursue opportunities aligned with our natural inclinations. By identifying and appreciating our strengths, we can set meaningful goals and make choices that bring out the best in us.

Recognizing and embracing your strengths and weaknesses is a crucial aspect of self-awareness and personal growth. Here's why it is important and how you can effectively approach it:

1. Self-confidence and self-acceptance: Recognizing your strengths allows you to build self-confidence and develop a positive self-image. Embracing your strengths means acknowledging your unique qualities, skills, and talents, which can boost your self-esteem. Similarly, acknowledging your weaknesses with self-acceptance enables you to embrace your imperfections and work towards self-improvement without harsh self-criticism.
2. Effective goal setting: Understanding your strengths helps you set realistic and achievable goals. By

leveraging your strengths, you can align your goals with your natural abilities and increase the likelihood of success. Conversely, recognizing your weaknesses helps you identify areas where you may need additional support or development to achieve your goals.

3. Improved self-awareness: Recognizing both your strengths and weaknesses enhances self-awareness. It allows you to have a realistic understanding of your capabilities and limitations. This self-awareness enables you to make informed decisions, capitalize on your strengths, and seek assistance or growth opportunities where needed.
4. Personal and professional development: Embracing your strengths empowers you to further develop and refine them. By focusing on your areas of expertise, you can enhance your skills, deepen your knowledge, and become a more valuable asset in various areas of your life. Similarly, acknowledging your weaknesses opens the door for growth and improvement. It enables you to seek opportunities for learning, skill development, and personal growth.
5. Effective teamwork and collaboration: Recognizing your strengths and weaknesses facilitates effective teamwork and collaboration with others. It allows you to contribute your strengths to a team, which can lead to better outcomes and synergy. Additionally, acknowledging your weaknesses enables you to seek support from others who possess complementary strengths, fostering a more balanced and productive collaborative environment.
6. Adaptability and resilience: Being aware of your strengths and weaknesses allows you to adapt to different situations and challenges. You can leverage your strengths in areas where you excel, while acknowledging your weaknesses helps you identify

areas that require growth or alternative strategies. This adaptability and resilience are essential for navigating through life's ups and downs with confidence and agility.

To effectively recognize and embrace your strengths and weaknesses:

Embracing our strengths involves fully accepting and utilizing them to achieve success and fulfilment. When we embrace our strengths, we cultivate a sense of self-assurance and authenticity. We can focus on activities that align with our strengths, which leads to increased motivation, productivity, and enjoyment. By embracing our strengths, we create a path that capitalizes on our unique qualities and leads to greater satisfaction in our personal and professional lives.

Recognizing our weaknesses is equally important as it provides an opportunity for growth and development. Being aware of areas where we may have limitations or room for improvement allows us to take proactive steps to enhance those aspects of ourselves. By acknowledging our weaknesses without judgment or self-criticism, we can approach them with a growth Mind-set and view them as opportunities for learning and progress.

Embracing our weaknesses involves taking proactive measures to overcome them. This can include seeking additional education or training, seeking guidance or mentorship from experts, or developing strategies to improve in specific areas. By actively working on our weaknesses, we can expand our skill set, broaden our perspectives, and become more well-rounded individuals.

Recognizing and embracing both strengths and weaknesses is about finding balance. It is important to acknowledge that no one is perfect, and we all have areas for growth. Embracing our strengths while being aware of our weaknesses allows us to develop a holistic sense of self-awareness. It helps us cultivate humility, authenticity, and a willingness to continuously learn and improve.

1. Engage in self-reflection and introspection: Take time to reflect on your experiences, achievements, and areas where you excel. Similarly, reflect on situations where you may have struggled or encountered challenges.

2. Seek feedback: Ask for feedback from trusted friends, mentors, or colleagues to gain different perspectives on your strengths and weaknesses. Be open to constructive criticism and use it as an opportunity for growth.

3. Focus on growth and improvement: Embrace a growth Mind-set that acknowledges weaknesses as areas for improvement rather than fixed limitations. Develop strategies and seek resources that can help you enhance your strengths and address your weaknesses.

4. Embrace self-compassion: Be kind and patient with yourself as you navigate your strengths and weaknesses. Embrace self-compassion and understand that everyone has areas of strength and areas for growth.

Surrounding ourselves with a supportive network of individuals who recognize and appreciate our strengths and weaknesses can be invaluable. Trusted friends, mentors, or colleagues can offer valuable insights and feedback to help us further develop our strengths and address our weaknesses. Their support and encouragement can provide the motivation and accountability needed for personal growth and improvement.

Recognizing and embracing your strengths and weaknesses is a continuous process. Regular self-assessment, learning, and adaptation can help you leverage your strengths, work on areas of improvement, and ultimately thrive in various aspects of your life.

Recognizing and embracing our strengths and weaknesses is a journey of self-discovery and personal growth. By acknowledging and leveraging our strengths, we can tap into our unique potential and pursue success with confidence. Simultaneously, by embracing our weaknesses, we open ourselves up to growth, learning, and personal development. The key lies in finding a balance, accepting ourselves as multidimensional individuals, and actively working towards self-improvement. Through self-awareness and a supportive network, we can navigate this journey of recognizing and embracing our strengths and weaknesses, unlocking our full potential, and living a fulfilling and authentic life.

Identifying Limiting Beliefs and Self-sabotaging Patterns

Limiting beliefs and self-sabotaging patterns can significantly hinder our personal growth, success, and overall well-being. These negative thought patterns and behaviors often stem from deep-seated beliefs that hold us back from realizing our full potential. Identifying limiting beliefs and self-sabotaging patterns is an important step in personal growth and overcoming obstacles. Here's how you can recognize and address them:

1. Self-reflection and introspection: Take time to reflect on your thoughts, beliefs, and behaviors. Notice any recurring patterns or negative self-talk that may be holding you back. Consider situations where you may have undermined your own success or happiness.
2. Question your beliefs: Challenge the beliefs that limit you. Ask yourself if they are based on facts or if they are simply assumptions or self-imposed restrictions. Evaluate the evidence that supports or contradicts these beliefs. Often, you will find that many limiting beliefs are unfounded or based on outdated information.

3. Pay attention to self-sabotaging behaviors: Notice if you engage in self-sabotaging behaviors that undermine your progress or success. Examples include procrastination, self-doubt, perfectionism, fear of failure, or self-sabotaging relationships. Awareness of these behaviors is the first step toward changing them.
4. Seek external perspectives: Talk to trusted friends, mentors, or therapists who can provide objective insights and help you identify blind spots or self-sabotaging patterns that you may not see on your own.
5. Challenge negative self-talk: Pay attention to your inner dialogue and challenge negative self-talk. Replace self-defeating thoughts with more positive and empowering ones. Practice self-compassion and cultivate a Mind-set of self-belief and self-encouragement.
6. Explore the origins of limiting beliefs: Consider where your limiting beliefs may have originated. They can stem from past experiences, societal conditioning, childhood influences, or negative feedback from others. Understanding their roots can help you disentangle yourself from their grip.
7. Reframe and reframe beliefs: Once you have identified limiting beliefs, work on reframing them. Replace negative beliefs with positive and empowering alternatives. Focus on evidence that supports your growth and capabilities. Affirmations, visualizations, and positive self-talk can support this process.
8. Take small steps and celebrate progress: Overcoming limiting beliefs and self-sabotaging patterns is a gradual process. Start by taking small steps outside your comfort zone and gradually expand your boundaries. Celebrate each milestone and acknowledge your progress along the way.
9. Surround yourself with positive influences: Surround yourself with supportive and positive people who

believe in your potential. Seek out communities, mentors, or role models who can inspire and uplift you. Their encouragement and guidance can help you challenge and overcome limiting beliefs.

10. Understanding Limiting Beliefs: Limiting beliefs are negative and restrictive thoughts that we hold about ourselves, others, or the world around us. These beliefs often stem from past experiences, societal conditioning, or fear of failure. Common limiting beliefs include thoughts such as "I'm not good enough," "I don't deserve success," or "I'm destined to fail." These beliefs create self-doubt, hinder progress, and limit our ability to take risks and pursue our goals.

11. The Impact of Self-Sabotaging Patterns: Self-sabotaging patterns are destructive behaviors or actions that undermine our own success or well-being. These patterns can manifest as procrastination, self-destructive habits, perfectionism, fear of success, or fear of failure. Engaging in self-sabotage prevents us from achieving our goals and living up to our true potential. Understanding and addressing these patterns is crucial for personal growth and achieving long-term success.

12. Recognizing Limiting Beliefs and Self-Sabotaging Patterns: Becoming aware of our limiting beliefs and self-sabotaging patterns is the first step in breaking free from their grip. Paying attention to recurring negative thoughts, self-critical inner dialogue, and repetitive behaviors that hinder progress can help identify these patterns. Journaling, self-reflection, and seeking feedback from trusted individuals can provide valuable insights into our limiting beliefs and self-sabotaging tendencies.

13. Challenging and Reframing Limiting Beliefs: Once identified, it is important to challenge and reframe our limiting beliefs. This involves questioning the validity

of these beliefs and replacing them with more empowering and supportive thoughts. Practicing positive affirmations, gathering evidence of our accomplishments and capabilities, and surrounding ourselves with positive influences can help shift our Mind-set and replace limiting beliefs with more empowering ones.

14. Breaking Self-Sabotaging Patterns: Breaking self-sabotaging patterns requires a combination of self-awareness, self-discipline, and self-compassion. Identifying the triggers, emotions, and underlying reasons behind these patterns is crucial. Developing strategies such as setting realistic goals, creating accountability systems, practicing self-care, and seeking support from others can aid in breaking these patterns and fostering healthier behaviors and habits.

15. Cultivating a Growth Mind-set: Cultivating a growth Mind-set is essential in overcoming limiting beliefs and self-sabotaging patterns. Embracing the belief that our abilities and intelligence can be developed through effort and learning allows us to approach challenges with resilience and a willingness to learn from setbacks. By adopting a growth Mind-set, we open ourselves up to new possibilities, embrace challenges as opportunities for growth, and persist in the face of obstacles.

Identifying and addressing limiting beliefs and self-sabotaging patterns is crucial for personal growth, success, and fulfilment. By recognizing these negative thought patterns and behaviors, challenging and reframing limiting beliefs, and breaking self-sabotaging patterns, we can free ourselves from their constraints. Embracing a growth mind-set, practicing self-compassion, and seeking support from others are key elements in this transformative journey. By releasing limiting beliefs and self-sabotage, we open ourselves up to new opportunities.

Remember that identifying and addressing limiting beliefs and self-sabotaging patterns takes time and effort. Be patient with yourself and commit to consistent self-reflection and personal growth. As you let go of these obstacles, you open up space for personal transformation and the realization of your full potential.

3

The Mind-Body Connection: Nurturing a Positive Self-Image

The mind and body are intricately connected, and nurturing a positive self-image is essential for overall well-being and a fulfilling life. When we cultivate a healthy relationship between our mind and body, we enhance our self-esteem, boost our confidence, and improve our overall quality of life.

The mind-body connection refers to the relationship between our mental and emotional states and our physical well-being. It suggests that our thoughts, feelings, beliefs, and attitudes can influence our physical health and vice versa. Here are some key aspects of the mind-body connection:

1. Stress and the immune system: Research has shown that chronic stress and negative emotions can weaken the immune system, making individuals more susceptible to illnesses and diseases. Conversely, positive emotions and relaxation techniques have been found to support immune function and overall health.
2. Psychosomatic symptoms: Psychosomatic symptoms are physical symptoms that are caused or influenced by psychological factors. For example, stress or anxiety can manifest as headaches, digestive issues, muscle tension, or fatigue. Understanding the connection between the mind and body can help individuals address the underlying psychological factors contributing to their physical symptoms.
3. Placebo effect: The placebo effect demonstrates the

power of belief and expectation on health outcomes. When individuals believe they are receiving a treatment, even if it is a placebo (a non-active substance), they may experience improvements in their symptoms. This highlights the influence of our mind and beliefs on our physical well-being.

4. Mindfulness and pain management: Mindfulness practices, such as meditation and deep breathing, have been shown to reduce pain perception and improve pain management. By directing attention to the present moment and cultivating non-judgmental awareness, individuals can experience relief from physical discomfort.

5. Emotions and cardiovascular health: Emotions like anger, stress, and hostility have been linked to an increased risk of cardiovascular problems, including high blood pressure, heart disease, and stroke. On the other hand, positive emotions, such as happiness and gratitude, have been associated with better cardiovascular health and improved overall well-being.

6. Gut-brain connection: The gut-brain axis highlights the bidirectional communication between the brain and the gastrointestinal system. Emotional states can impact gut health, and disturbances in gut health can influence mood and mental well-being. This connection emphasizes the importance of maintaining a healthy gut through nutrition, stress management, and lifestyle choices.

7. Mind-body practices: Various mind-body practices, such as yoga, tai chi, and qigong, promote the integration of mind and body. These practices combine physical movements, breathwork, and mindfulness to enhance overall well-being, reduce stress, improve flexibility, and cultivate a sense of inner balance.

8. Mind-body medicine: Mind-body medicine approaches, such as meditation, relaxation techniques, guided imagery, and cognitive-behavioral therapy, are used to complement traditional medical treatments. These approaches recognize the influence of the mind on physical health and aim to harness the mind-body connection for healing and well-being.
9. Understanding the Mind-Body Connection:\ The mind and body are interconnected systems that constantly influence each other. Our thoughts, beliefs, and emotions can impact our physical well-being, while our physical health can affect our mental and emotional state. Recognizing this connection allows us to harness its power to cultivate a positive self-image.
10. Practicing Self-Care: Self-care plays a crucial role in nurturing a positive self-image. Taking care of our physical health through regular exercise, proper nutrition, and sufficient rest helps improve our energy levels, mood, and overall well-being. Engaging in activities that promote relaxation, such as mindfulness, meditation, or hobbies we enjoy, can also contribute to a positive self-image by reducing stress and promoting a sense of self-worth.
11. Cultivating Positive Body Image: Developing a positive body image involves accepting and appreciating our bodies as they are, regardless of societal ideals or standards. This includes embracing diversity, celebrating our unique features, and reframing negative self-talk. Engaging in activities that promote body positivity, such as practicing self-compassion, surrounding ourselves with body-positive influences, and focusing on what our bodies can do rather than how they look, can foster a healthy and positive self-image.
12. Challenging Negative Thoughts and Beliefs: Negative thoughts and beliefs can significantly impact our self-

image. It is essential to challenge and reframe these negative thoughts by replacing them with positive and affirming ones. This can be achieved through cognitive-behavioral techniques, such as identifying and questioning negative beliefs, replacing them with more empowering thoughts, and practicing self-compassion and self-acceptance.

13. Surrounding Yourself with Positive Influences: Our environment and the people we surround ourselves with greatly influence our self-image. It is important to seek out positive and supportive relationships that uplift and encourage us. Surrounding ourselves with individuals who appreciate and celebrate our strengths, values, and uniqueness can contribute to a positive self-image. Additionally, seeking out positive and empowering media, books, or online content can help counteract negative societal messages and foster a healthier self-perception.

Understanding and nurturing the mind-body connection can have profound effects on our overall health and well-being. By cultivating positive thoughts, managing stress, practicing self-care, and incorporating mind-body practices into our lives, we can promote a harmonious relationship between our mental and physical states, leading to greater vitality and wellness.

Embracing Mindfulness and Self-Reflection

Embracing mindfulness and self-reflection can have transformative effects on your personal growth, well-being, and relationships. Here's how you can incorporate these practices into your life:

1. Mindfulness:

- Start with the present moment: Bring your awareness to the here and now. Notice your thoughts, emotions, and sensations without judgment. Cultivate a sense of curiosity and openness to whatever arises in the present moment.

- Practice formal meditation: Set aside dedicated time each day for mindfulness meditation. Find a quiet space, sit comfortably, and focus your attention on your breath, bodily sensations, or a specific anchor point. When your mind wanders, gently bring it back to the present moment.
- Engage in informal mindfulness: Extend mindfulness into your daily activities. Pay attention to the sensations of eating, walking, or performing routine tasks. Be fully present and engaged in each moment, rather than being caught up in autopilot mode.
- Acceptance and non-judgment: Practice accepting things as they are, including your thoughts, emotions, and experiences. Avoid labeling them as good or bad. Cultivate a non-judgmental attitude and approach each moment with curiosity and compassion.
- Gratitude and appreciation: Take time to cultivate gratitude for the present moment and the experiences and people in your life. Notice and appreciate the simple joys, blessings, and acts of kindness that surround you.

2. Self-Reflection:

- Journaling: Set aside regular time for reflective writing. Use a journal to explore your thoughts, feelings, and experiences. Reflect on your goals, values, and challenges. Writing can help clarify your thoughts, gain insights, and track your progress.
- Ask reflective questions: Challenge yourself with thought-provoking questions. What are your strengths and areas for growth? What brings you joy and fulfillment? What patterns or beliefs may be holding you back? What steps can you take to align your actions with your values?

- Seek solitude: Carve out moments of solitude and silence to reconnect with yourself. Disconnect from distractions, technology, and external noise. Use this time for introspection, self-observation, and reconnecting with your inner voice.
- Seek feedback: Request feedback from trusted friends, family members, or mentors. Ask for their observations and insights on your strengths, blind spots, and areas for improvement. Be open to receiving constructive criticism and use it as an opportunity for growth.
- Learn from experiences: Reflect on past experiences, both positive and negative. Identify lessons learned, insights gained, and areas where you can grow. Consider how you can apply these lessons to future situations and make adjustments accordingly.

Both mindfulness and self-reflection require practice and consistency. Start with small steps and gradually integrate these practices into your daily life. Embracing mindfulness and self-reflection can deepen your self-awareness, enhance your emotional well-being, and lead to greater clarity, fulfillment, and meaningful connections with yourself and others.

Practicing mindfulness and self-reflection allows us to become more attuned to our thoughts, emotions, and physical sensations. By cultivating present-moment awareness, we can observe and acknowledge any negative self-image patterns or self-critical thoughts that arise. Through self-reflection, we can explore the underlying causes of these thoughts and develop strategies to nurture a more positive self-image.

Nurturing a positive self-image through the mind-body connection is a transformative and ongoing process. By recognizing the impact of our thoughts, beliefs, and physical well-being on our self-image, we can actively work towards cultivating a healthier and more positive perception of ourselves. Through self-care, positive body image, challenging negative thoughts, surrounding ourselves with positive influences, and practicing mindfulness and self-reflection, we can foster a strong sense of self-worth, confidence, and fulfillment. Embracing a positive self-image allows us to live authentically, embrace our uniqueness, and pursue a life of happiness and self-actualization.

Understanding the Mind-body Connection and Its Impact on Confidence

The mind-body connection refers to the intricate relationship between our thoughts, emotions, and physical well-being. Understanding this connection is essential in building and maintaining confidence. When we nurture a harmonious relationship between our mind and body, we can cultivate a deep sense of self-assurance and belief in our abilities.

The mind-body connection can have a significant impact on confidence. Here's how the two are interconnected:

1. Self-perception and body language: Our thoughts, emotions, and beliefs about ourselves can manifest in our body language and physical presence. When we feel confident, our body language tends to be more open, upright, and expressive. Conversely, when we lack confidence, our body language may become closed, slouched, or tense. By becoming aware of our body language and intentionally adjusting it, we can influence our mental state and boost our confidence.

2. Positive self-talk: The way we talk to ourselves internally can greatly impact our confidence. Negative self-talk, such as self-criticism, self-doubt, or self-sabotaging thoughts, can erode confidence. On the other hand, positive self-talk and affirmations can nurture self-belief, challenge limiting beliefs, and foster a confident Mind-set. By cultivating positive thoughts and reframing negative self-talk, we can strengthen our confidence.

3. Physiology and confidence: Our physical state can influence our mental and emotional states. Engaging in activities that promote physical well-being, such as exercise, adequate sleep, and healthy nutrition, can positively impact our mood, energy levels, and overall confidence. Taking care of our bodies can provide a solid foundation for cultivating confidence.

4. Confidence and risk-taking: Confidence is closely linked to our willingness to take risks and step out of our comfort zones. When we have confidence in our abilities and believe in ourselves, we are more likely to embrace challenges, seize opportunities, and take calculated risks. This, in turn, can lead to personal growth, increased competence, and further boosts in confidence.

5. Mindfulness and self-compassion: Mindfulness practices can help us observe and manage our thoughts and emotions, including self-doubt and insecurity. By practicing non-judgmental awareness, we can acknowledge our insecurities without letting them define us. Additionally, cultivating self-compassion and treating ourselves with kindness and understanding can counteract self-critical thoughts and enhance self-confidence.

6. Feedback and learning: Confidence can be nurtured through learning and seeking feedback. Actively pursuing new skills, seeking opportunities for growth, and embracing a growth Mind-set can boost confidence. By seeking feedback from others and using it constructively, we can gain valuable insights, refine our abilities, and strengthen our belief in our capabilities.

7. Mind-Body Unity: The mind and body are not separate entities but rather interconnected aspects of our being. Our thoughts and emotions have a profound impact on our physical state, and vice versa. Recognizing this unity allows us to harness the power of our thoughts and physical sensations to enhance our confidence.

8. Positive Thinking and Self-Talk: Our thoughts and self-talk significantly influence our confidence levels. Positive thinking involves consciously shifting our focus towards empowering and supportive thoughts. By cultivating an optimistic and self-affirming Mind-set, we can build confidence and belief in our abilities. Practicing positive self-talk involves replacing self-doubt and self-criticism with encouraging and uplifting inner dialogue.
9. Body Language and Posture: Our body language and posture not only reflect our confidence but also affect our internal state. Adopting an open and expansive posture, such as standing tall, making eye contact, and having a relaxed demeanor, can influence our emotions and instill a sense of confidence. Conversely, slouching or closed-off body language can reinforce negative emotions and self-doubt. By consciously aligning our body language with confidence, we can positively impact our Mind-set.
10. Movement and Exercise: Physical movement and exercise have a direct impact on our mental and emotional well-being. Engaging in regular exercise releases endorphins, which promote feelings of happiness and positivity. Additionally, physical activity improves self-perception, body image, and overall self-esteem. Incorporating movement into our daily routine, whether through exercise, dance, yoga, or any other enjoyable activity, can boost confidence by nurturing the mind-body connection.
11. Breath and Relaxation Techniques: Our breath is a powerful tool for regulating our emotions and promoting relaxation. Deep, conscious breathing activates the parasympathetic nervous system, inducing a state of calm and reducing stress. By incorporating breathwork and relaxation techniques, such as deep

breathing exercises, meditation, or mindfulness, we can cultivate a sense of inner calmness, clarity, and confidence.

12. Self-Care and Well-being: Nurturing our overall well-being through self-care practices positively impacts our confidence. Prioritizing self-care involves attending to our physical, emotional, and mental needs. Engaging in activities that promote relaxation, stress reduction, and personal fulfillment, such as hobbies, self-reflection, or quality time with loved ones, enhances our self-esteem and reinforces a positive mind-body connection.

The mind-body connection plays a vital role in shaping our confidence and belief in ourselves. By understanding and nurturing this connection, we can harness its power to cultivate a deep sense of self-assurance and belief in our abilities. Through positive thinking, affirming self-talk, confident body language, movement and exercise, breath and relaxation techniques, and self-care practices, we can strengthen our confidence and create a solid foundation for personal growth and success. Embracing the mind-body connection allows us to tap into our inner potential, overcome self-doubt, and navigate life with unwavering confidence.

Overall, the mind-body connection plays a vital role in confidence. By nurturing positive thoughts, taking care of our physical well-being, practicing mindfulness, and engaging in self-compassion, we can enhance our confidence levels. Recognizing the impact of our thoughts, emotions, and physical state on confidence allows us to actively shape and cultivate our self-belief and overall sense of empowerment.

Practicing Self-care and Self-compassion

Self-care and self-compassion are essential components of nurturing our well-being and cultivating a healthy relationship with ourselves. These practices involve prioritizing our physical, emotional, and mental needs, and treating ourselves with kindness and understanding. By embracing self-care and self-compassion, we can enhance our overall happiness, resilience, and self-esteem.

Practicing self-care and self-compassion are essential for maintaining overall well-being and cultivating a positive relationship with oneself. Here's how you can incorporate these practices into your life:

1. Prioritize your needs: Take time to identify your needs and make them a priority. This may involve setting boundaries, saying no when necessary, and carving out time for activities that bring you joy and relaxation.
2. Physical self-care: Take care of your physical well-being by engaging in regular exercise, eating nourishing foods, getting enough sleep, and attending to any medical needs. Pay attention to your body's signals and give it the care and attention it deserves.
3. Emotional self-care: Allow yourself to experience and process your emotions. Practice self-compassion by acknowledging your feelings without judgment or self-criticism. Engage in activities that support emotional well-being, such as journaling, talking to a trusted friend, practicing mindfulness, or engaging in creative outlets.
4. Set boundaries: Establishing boundaries is crucial for self-care. Learn to say no to activities or commitments that deplete your energy or do not align with your values. Communicate your boundaries clearly and assertively, and respect the boundaries of others.
5. Practice self-compassion: Treat yourself with kindness, understanding, and acceptance. Embrace your imperfections and recognize that everyone makes mistakes and faces challenges. Offer yourself the same compassion and support you would offer a loved one in difficult times.

6. Engage in activities you enjoy: Set aside time for activities that bring you joy and relaxation. Engaging in hobbies, pursuing creative outlets, spending time in nature, or practicing mindfulness can help you recharge and reconnect with yourself.
7. Practice self-reflection: Regularly reflect on your thoughts, emotions, and experiences. Cultivate self-awareness and explore any negative self-talk or limiting beliefs that may hinder self-care and self-compassion. Challenge those thoughts and replace them with more supportive and empowering ones.
8. Surround yourself with positive influences: Seek out relationships and communities that support and uplift you. Surrounding yourself with positive and supportive people can contribute to your overall well-being and reinforce self-care and self-compassion.
9. Seek support when needed: Don't hesitate to seek support from trusted friends, family, or professionals when you need it. Asking for help is a sign of strength and self-awareness. Reach out to individuals who can provide guidance, empathy, and encouragement.
10. Understanding Self-Care: Self-care refers to the deliberate and intentional actions we take to nurture our physical, emotional, and mental well-being. It involves recognizing and prioritizing our needs and engaging in activities that promote self-nurturing, relaxation, and rejuvenation. Self-care is about valuing ourselves enough to make our well-being a priority.
11. The Importance of Self-Compassion: Self-compassion is the practice of treating ourselves with kindness, understanding, and acceptance, especially in times of difficulty or self-judgment. It involves acknowledging our imperfections, mistakes, and struggles with a sense of empathy and non-judgment. Self-compassion allows

us to embrace our humanity and foster a nurturing relationship with ourselves.

12. Physical Self-Care: Physical self-care involves taking care of our body's needs to promote overall well-being. This includes getting sufficient restful sleep, maintaining a balanced and nutritious diet, engaging in regular physical activity, and attending to our physical health needs. Physical self-care supports our energy levels, vitality, and overall functioning.

13. Emotional Self-Care: Emotional self-care focuses on nurturing our emotional well-being and managing our emotions effectively. This includes recognizing and expressing our feelings, engaging in activities that bring us joy and fulfillment, and setting boundaries to protect our emotional well-being. Emotional self-care involves self-reflection, seeking support from others, and practicing emotional resilience.

14. Mental Self-Care: Mental self-care involves prioritizing activities that support our mental well-being and cognitive functioning. This includes engaging in activities that stimulate our minds, such as reading, learning new skills, or engaging in creative pursuits. Mental self-care also involves setting healthy boundaries with technology, managing stress, and practicing mindfulness or meditation to cultivate a calm and focused Mind-set.

15. Cultivating Self-Compassion: Practicing self-compassion involves treating ourselves with kindness, understanding, and acceptance, just as we would treat a close friend or loved one. It includes offering ourselves words of encouragement, acknowledging our efforts and progress, and embracing self-acceptance. Cultivating self-compassion involves challenging our inner critic, practicing self-forgiveness, and offering ourselves grace in times of difficulty or setbacks.

16. Integrating Self-Care and Self-Compassion: Integrating self-care and self-compassion involves recognizing that we deserve care, kindness, and understanding from ourselves. It means prioritizing our well-being and practicing self-compassion as we engage in self-care activities. By combining these practices, we create a strong foundation of self-love, resilience, and inner peace.

Practicing self-care and self-compassion is a transformative journey of nurturing our well-being and building a loving relationship with ourselves. By prioritizing our physical, emotional, and mental needs, and treating ourselves with kindness, understanding, and acceptance, we enhance our overall happiness, resilience, and self-esteem. Through physical self-care, emotional self-care, mental self-care, and cultivating self-compassion, we create a foundation for personal growth, well-being, and a fulfilling life.

Remember that self-care and self-compassion are ongoing practices that require consistency and intention. Be patient with yourself and embrace these practices as acts of self-love and self-nurturing. By prioritizing your well-being and cultivating self-compassion, you can enhance your overall happiness, resilience, and ability to navigate life's challenges with grace and self-acceptance.

Cultivating a Positive Self-image Through Physical and Mental Well-being

Cultivating a positive self-image involves nurturing our physical and mental well-being. When we prioritize our physical health and engage in practices that support our mental well-being, we can develop a strong and positive perception of ourselves. Cultivating a positive self-image involves nurturing both physical and mental well-being. The connection between physical and mental well-being and discuss strategies for cultivating a positive self-image through these avenues.

Cultivating a positive self-image involves nurturing both physical and mental well-being. Here are some practices that can help in this process:

Physical Well-being:

1. Regular exercise: Engage in physical activities that you enjoy and that make you feel good. Exercise not only promotes physical health but also releases endorphins, which can boost mood and enhance self-confidence.
2. Nourishing diet: Eat a balanced and nourishing diet that fuels your body and provides the necessary nutrients. Focus on whole foods, fruits, vegetables, lean proteins, and healthy fats. A healthy diet can contribute to increased energy levels, improved physical health, and a positive body image.
3. Adequate sleep: Prioritize getting enough sleep to support physical and mental rejuvenation. Lack of sleep can impact mood, cognitive function, and overall well-being. Establish a consistent sleep routine and create a sleep-friendly environment for quality rest.
4. Personal hygiene: Take care of your personal hygiene by engaging in regular grooming and self-care practices. This can contribute to feeling clean, refreshed, and confident in your physical appearance.

Mental Well-being:

1. Positive self-talk: Be mindful of your inner dialogue and consciously replace self-critical thoughts with positive and encouraging ones. Challenge negative self-perceptions and focus on your strengths, accomplishments, and unique qualities.
2. Practice gratitude: Cultivate a Mind-set of gratitude by acknowledging and appreciating the positive aspects of your life. Reflect on the things you are grateful for, both internally and externally, and express gratitude

regularly. This can enhance your overall outlook and boost self-esteem.

3. Set realistic goals: Set realistic and achievable goals that align with your values and aspirations. Break them down into smaller steps, celebrate progress along the way, and acknowledge your achievements. This can build confidence and a sense of accomplishment.
4. Surround yourself with positivity: Surround yourself with supportive and positive influences, including friends, family, and mentors who uplift and encourage you. Minimize exposure to negative or toxic environments that may hinder your self-image.
5. Engage in self-reflection and self-acceptance: Regularly reflect on your thoughts, beliefs, and emotions. Cultivate self-awareness and self-acceptance, embracing your strengths, weaknesses, and imperfections. Recognize that everyone has flaws and that self-acceptance is a journey.
6. Seek professional support: If you are struggling with self-image or mental well-being, consider seeking support from a mental health professional. They can provide guidance, tools, and techniques to help you cultivate a positive self-image and address any underlying challenges.

Remember that cultivating a positive self-image is an on-going process that requires self-care, self-compassion, and patience. Be kind to yourself, celebrate your uniqueness, and focus on holistic well-being. By nurturing both your physical and mental well-being, you can foster a positive self-image and embrace your true worth.

1. The Link between Physical and Mental Well-Being: Physical and mental well-being are deeply intertwined. Taking care of our physical health can have a profound impact on our mental state, and vice versa. Engaging

in activities that promote both physical and mental well-being is key to fostering a positive self-image.

2. Prioritizing Physical Well-Being: Physical well-being involves taking care of our bodies through healthy lifestyle choices. This includes regular exercise, proper nutrition, adequate sleep, and regular medical check-ups. Prioritizing physical well-being enhances our energy levels, boosts self-confidence, and promotes a positive self-image.

3. Engaging in Regular Exercise: Exercise is not only beneficial for our physical health but also plays a significant role in our mental well-being. Physical activity releases endorphins, which are natural mood boosters. Engaging in regular exercise, whether it's through cardiovascular activities, strength training, or yoga, can improve our self-image by enhancing our overall fitness, body strength, and body positivity.

4. Nurturing Mental Well-Being: Cultivating a positive self-image requires paying attention to our mental well-being. This involves managing stress, practicing mindfulness or meditation, seeking support when needed, and engaging in activities that promote relaxation and self-reflection. Nurturing our mental well-being helps reduce negative self-talk and fosters a positive Mind-set.

5. Building Resilience: Resilience is the ability to bounce back from challenges and setbacks. Developing resilience contributes to a positive self-image by allowing us to view difficulties as opportunities for growth rather than personal failures. Building resilience involves cultivating a positive Mind-set, setting realistic goals, practicing self-compassion, and seeking support from others when needed.

6. Challenging Negative Self-Talk: Negative self-talk can be detrimental to our self-image. It is important to

challenge and reframe negative thoughts and beliefs. By replacing self-criticism with self-encouragement and affirmations, we can cultivate a positive self-image and enhance our self-esteem.

7. Practicing Gratitude: Practicing gratitude involves focusing on the positive aspects of our lives and acknowledging the things we are grateful for. This practice helps shift our perspective towards the good and cultivates a positive self-image by fostering a sense of appreciation and contentment.

8. Surrounding Yourself with Positive Influences: The people we surround ourselves with greatly impact our self-image. Surrounding ourselves with supportive and positive individuals who appreciate and value us can reinforce our self-worth and contribute to a positive self-image. It is important to seek out relationships and communities that uplift and empower us.

Cultivating a positive self-image requires nurturing both our physical and mental well-being. By prioritizing physical health, engaging in regular exercise, nurturing our mental well-being, building resilience, challenging negative self-talk, practicing gratitude, and surrounding ourselves with positive influences, we can develop a strong and positive perception of ourselves. Embracing physical and mental well-being allows us to appreciate our bodies, enhance our self-confidence, and foster a positive self-image that empowers us to thrive in all aspects of life.

4

Rewriting Your Narrative: Transforming Limiting Beliefs

Rewriting your narrative refers to actively changing the way you perceive and tell your life story. It involves shifting your perspective, reframing past experiences, and creating a new narrative that empowers you and aligns with your values and aspirations. Here are some steps to help you in the process of rewriting your narrative:

1. Reflect on your current narrative: Take time to examine the story you have been telling yourself about your life, your abilities, and your experiences. Notice any negative or limiting beliefs that may be holding you back. Pay attention to recurring themes or patterns in your narrative.
2. Identify empowering themes: Identify empowering themes or aspects of your life that you want to highlight and incorporate into your new narrative. Look for strengths, accomplishments, lessons learned, and moments of growth or resilience. These can form the foundation of your revised narrative.
3. Challenge limiting beliefs: Identify any limiting beliefs or negative self-talk that have influenced your previous narrative. Question the validity of these beliefs and seek evidence to counteract them. Replace them with more empowering and supportive beliefs that align with your goals and aspirations.
4. Reframe past experiences: Take a fresh perspective on your past experiences. Look for alternative

interpretations or lessons that can be learned from challenging or difficult situations. Reframe them in a way that emphasizes personal growth, resilience, and the skills you have developed as a result.

5. Set new intentions and goals: Clarify your values, passions, and aspirations. Set new intentions and goals that align with the narrative you want to create for yourself. Focus on what you want to achieve and how you want to show up in the world. Define the steps you need to take to move towards your new narrative.
6. Practice self-compassion: Be gentle with yourself throughout this process. Recognize that rewriting your narrative takes time and effort. Practice self-compassion by treating yourself with kindness, patience, and understanding. Embrace self-care practices that support your emotional well-being.
7. Surround yourself with supportive influences: Surround yourself with people who support and encourage your new narrative. Seek out mentors, friends, or support groups that align with your values and aspirations. Engage in communities or activities that reinforce your positive narrative and provide a sense of belonging.
8. Practice affirmations and visualization: Use positive affirmations and visualization techniques to reinforce your new narrative. Affirmations are positive statements that reflect the narrative you want to adopt. Repeat them regularly and visualize yourself living out your new narrative in vivid detail.
9. Monitor and adjust: Regularly assess and monitor your narrative to ensure it continues to align with your evolving goals and values. Be open to adjusting and refining your narrative as you gain new experiences and insights. Embrace the growth and evolution that comes with rewriting your narrative.

Remember, rewriting your narrative is a personal and ongoing process. It requires self-reflection, self-awareness, and an active commitment to changing your Mind-set and perceptions. By consciously choosing and crafting your narrative, you can empower yourself, build resilience, and create a more fulfilling and authentic life story.

Our beliefs shape our reality, and often, we hold onto limiting beliefs that hinder our growth, success, and self-esteem. These beliefs create a narrative that defines how we perceive ourselves and the world around us. However, it is within our power to rewrite our narrative and transform these limiting beliefs into empowering ones.

1. Understanding Limiting Beliefs: Limiting beliefs are deeply ingrained thoughts and beliefs that hold us back from reaching our full potential. They often stem from past experiences, societal conditioning, or negative self-perception. Recognizing these beliefs is the first step in transforming them.
2. Identifying Limiting Beliefs: To rewrite our narrative, we must first identify the limiting beliefs that are holding us back. This requires self-reflection and self-awareness. We can examine patterns of negative self-talk, self-sabotaging behaviors, or areas where we feel stuck or limited. By exploring these areas, we can uncover the underlying beliefs that need to be transformed.
3. Challenging Limiting Beliefs: Once we have identified our limiting beliefs, we can begin to challenge them. We need to question their validity and examine the evidence supporting or refuting them. Often, we find that these beliefs are based on misconceptions or outdated information. By challenging their accuracy, we create space for new, empowering beliefs to emerge.
4. Reframing and Rewriting the Narrative: After challenging limiting beliefs, it is important to reframe

and rewrite our narrative. We can consciously choose new beliefs that align with our values, goals, and aspirations. This involves replacing negative self-talk with positive affirmations, visualizing success and positive outcomes, and creating a new narrative that supports our growth and self-esteem.

5. Building a Supportive Environment: Transforming limiting beliefs requires a supportive environment. Surrounding ourselves with individuals who believe in our potential and support our growth is crucial. Seeking guidance from mentors, coaches, or therapists can also provide valuable insights and tools for rewriting our narrative.
6. Taking Action and Embracing Growth: Rewriting our narrative is not just a mental exercise; it requires action. We need to step outside our comfort zone and take small, consistent steps towards our goals and aspirations. Each action we take reinforces our new beliefs and helps solidify our positive self-image.
7. Practicing Self-Compassion: Throughout the process of transforming limiting beliefs, it is important to practice self-compassion. We must be patient with ourselves, recognizing that change takes time. Embracing self-compassion allows us to be gentle and understanding as we navigate the journey of rewriting our narrative.
8. Embracing Continuous Growth: Transforming limiting beliefs is an ongoing process. As we continue to grow and evolve, new beliefs may surface that need to be addressed. Embracing a Mind-set of continuous growth allows us to remain open to new possibilities, challenge old beliefs, and rewrite our narrative as needed.

By recognizing, challenging, and rewriting our limiting beliefs, we can transform our narrative and create a new reality rooted in empowerment, self-belief, and personal growth. Through self-reflection, challenging beliefs, reframing our narrative, building a supportive environment, taking action, practicing self-compassion, and embracing continuous growth, we can rewrite our narrative to align with our true potential. By doing so, we cultivate a positive self-image and open the door to endless possibilities for success and fulfillment.

Recognizing and Challenging Negative Self-talk

Negative self-talk refers to the critical or self-defeating thoughts and beliefs we have about ourselves. It can significantly impact our self-esteem, confidence, and overall well-being. Recognizing and challenging negative self-talk is crucial for cultivating a more positive and supportive inner dialogue. Here are some steps to help you in this process:

1. Awareness: Start by becoming aware of your negative self-talk. Pay attention to the thoughts that arise in different situations or when faced with challenges. Notice the specific words, phrases, or recurring themes that contribute to negative self-talk.
2. Question the evidence: Challenge the validity of your negative thoughts by questioning the evidence supporting them. Ask yourself, "Is there concrete evidence to support this belief?" or "What are some alternative explanations or perspectives?"
3. Reality-check: Evaluate the accuracy of your negative thoughts. Are they based on facts or distorted perceptions? Consider whether your thoughts are an accurate reflection of who you are or if they are influenced by biases, past experiences, or unhelpful comparisons.
4. Reframe and reframe again: Replace negative thoughts with more realistic and empowering statements. Reframe negative self-talk into positive or neutral self-talk. For example, instead of saying, "I always mess things up," reframe it as, "I am capable of learning from my mistakes and improving."

5. Practice self-compassion: Treat yourself with kindness and understanding. Replace self-critical thoughts with self-compassionate ones. Remind yourself that it's okay to make mistakes, that everyone has flaws, and that you deserve compassion and self-care.

6. Use affirmations: Utilize positive affirmations to counteract negative self-talk. Create a list of affirmations that resonate with you and reflect your desired self-image. Repeat these affirmations regularly, especially when you catch yourself engaging in negative self-talk.

7. Seek support: Reach out to trusted friends, family, or professionals for support and perspective. Share your negative self-talk patterns with them and ask for their feedback and encouragement. They can provide objective viewpoints and remind you of your strengths and worth.

8. Gratitude and self-appreciation: Cultivate gratitude for your strengths, accomplishments, and the positive aspects of your life. Practice self-appreciation by acknowledging your efforts and progress. Celebrate small victories and focus on your positive attributes.

9. Practice mindfulness: Develop mindfulness skills to observe your thoughts without judgment. When negative self-talk arises, consciously acknowledge it and let it pass without getting entangled in the thoughts. Bring your attention back to the present moment and redirect your focus towards more positive or constructive thinking.

10. Persistence and patience: Changing negative self-talk patterns takes time and persistence. Be patient with yourself and understand that it's a process of rewiring your thinking patterns. Consistently challenge and replace negative self-talk with more supportive and empowering thoughts.

Remember that breaking the cycle of negative self-talk requires effort and practice. Be compassionate with yourself during this journey, as it takes time to develop new habits and thought patterns. With persistence and self-awareness, you can gradually transform negative self-talk into a more positive and nurturing inner dialogue.

Negative self-talk is the inner dialogue that undermines our confidence, self-esteem, and overall well-being. It often manifests as self-criticism, self-doubt, and harsh judgments towards ourselves. Recognizing and challenging negative self-talk is crucial for cultivating a positive self-image and nurturing our mental and emotional well-being.

1. Understanding Negative Self-Talk: Negative self-talk is the internal narrative of self-criticism, self-doubt, and negativity that influences our perception of ourselves and our abilities. It can stem from past experiences, societal influences, or internalized beliefs. Recognizing the impact of negative self-talk is the first step towards transforming it.
2. Identifying Negative Self-Talk Patterns: To challenge negative self-talk, we must first become aware of its presence in our thoughts. Paying attention to our internal dialogue and observing patterns of self-criticism and negativity can help us identify when negative self-talk arises. Journaling, mindfulness, and self-reflection can be valuable tools for uncovering these patterns.
3. Questioning the Validity of Negative Thoughts: Once we have identified negative self-talk, it is essential to question its validity. We can examine the evidence supporting or refuting these thoughts. Often, we find that negative self-talk is based on distorted perceptions or unfounded assumptions. By challenging its accuracy, we can begin to replace it with more realistic and empowering thoughts.

4. Practicing Self-Compassion: Self-compassion plays a crucial role in challenging negative self-talk. It involves treating ourselves with kindness, understanding, and acceptance, even in moments of self-doubt or perceived failure. Cultivating self-compassion allows us to counteract negative self-talk with self-nurturing and self-encouragement.

5. Reframing Negative Thoughts: Reframing negative thoughts involves consciously replacing them with more positive and empowering alternatives. By reframing negative statements into more balanced and realistic ones, we can shift our perspective and cultivate a more positive self-image. This process requires focusing on our strengths, achievements, and potential.

6. Using Affirmations and Positive Self-Talk: Affirmations and positive self-talk are powerful tools for challenging negative self-talk. Affirmations are positive statements that reflect our desired beliefs or qualities. By repeating affirmations regularly, we can rewire our thinking patterns and reinforce empowering thoughts. Engaging in positive self-talk involves consciously choosing supportive and encouraging language when speaking to ourselves.

7. Seeking Support: Challenging negative self-talk can be a challenging process. Seeking support from trusted friends, family members, or professionals, such as therapists or coaches, can provide valuable insights and encouragement. They can offer different perspectives, help us challenge distorted thinking, and provide guidance on developing healthier self-talk patterns.

8. Cultivating a Growth Mind-set: A growth Mind-set is the belief that our abilities and intelligence can be developed through effort, learning, and perseverance. By embracing a growth Mind-set, we view challenges and setbacks as opportunities for growth and learning,

rather than as reflections of our worth or abilities. Cultivating a growth Mind-set helps counteract negative self-talk and fosters a belief in our potential.

Recognizing and challenging negative self-talk is a transformative process that empowers us to cultivate a positive self-image and nurture our mental and emotional well-being. By becoming aware of negative self-talk patterns, questioning its validity, practicing self-compassion, reframing negative thoughts, using affirmations and positive self-talk, seeking support, and cultivating a growth Mind-set, we can break free from the constraints of

Examining the Origins of Limiting Beliefs

Examining the origins of limiting beliefs is an important step in understanding and overcoming them. Here are some approaches to explore the origins of your limiting beliefs:

1. Self-reflection: Take time to reflect on your beliefs and try to trace them back to their origins. Ask yourself questions like, "When did I first start believing this about myself?" or "What experiences or influences contributed to the formation of this belief?" Self-reflection can help uncover underlying experiences or conditioning that shaped your beliefs.
2. Childhood and upbringing: Examine the messages and experiences you received during your childhood and upbringing. Our early experiences, interactions with parents, caregivers, and significant others, as well as societal and cultural influences, can play a significant role in shaping our beliefs about ourselves and the world.
3. Significant life events: Reflect on significant life events or traumas that may have contributed to the formation of your limiting beliefs. These events could have reinforced negative beliefs or created new ones as a way

of protecting yourself from further pain or disappointment.

4. Cultural and societal influences: Consider the impact of cultural and societal beliefs and norms on your own belief system. These influences can shape our perceptions of what is possible or acceptable, leading to the adoption of limiting beliefs.

5. Comparison and external validation: Examine whether your limiting beliefs are influenced by comparing yourself to others or seeking external validation. Sometimes, we adopt limiting beliefs because we believe we don't measure up to certain standards set by society or others' opinions of us.

6. Feedback and criticism: Reflect on past feedback or criticism you have received. Negative feedback or criticism, especially when repeated or emphasized, can contribute to the formation of limiting beliefs. Consider whether external input has influenced your beliefs about yourself.

7. Personal interpretations: Explore how you have interpreted and made meaning of past experiences. Our interpretations of events can shape our beliefs and perceptions. Sometimes, we draw conclusions based on limited information or skewed perspectives, leading to the development of limiting beliefs.

8. Core fears and insecurities: Identify any core fears or insecurities that underlie your limiting beliefs. These core fears can stem from past experiences or feelings of inadequacy, rejection, or failure. Understanding these core fears can provide insight into the origins of your limiting beliefs.

9. Seeking professional help: If you find it challenging to identify the origins of your limiting beliefs on your own, consider seeking support from a therapist or counselor.

They can help you explore and understand the underlying factors contributing to your beliefs and provide guidance in overcoming them.

Remember that examining the origins of limiting beliefs is a process of self-discovery and self-compassion. It's important to approach this exploration with curiosity and without judgment. By gaining insight into the origins of your limiting beliefs, you can begin to challenge and reframe them, freeing yourself from their constraints and creating new empowering beliefs that better serve you. Limiting beliefs are deeply ingrained thoughts and beliefs that hinder our personal growth, success, and self-esteem. To effectively transform these beliefs, it is essential to understand their origins.

1. Childhood Experiences and Conditioning: Many limiting beliefs stem from our childhood experiences and the conditioning we received during that time. Messages we received from caregivers, teachers, and other influential figures can shape our beliefs about ourselves and our abilities. Examining the messages we internalized during childhood helps us identify the origins of our limiting beliefs.
2. Cultural and Societal Influences: Society and culture play a significant role in shaping our beliefs. We are exposed to societal standards, stereotypes, and expectations that can create limiting beliefs about our worth, capabilities, and potential. By examining the cultural and societal influences that have shaped our beliefs, we gain insight into the external factors that contribute to our self-perception.
3. Personal Experiences and Trauma: Limiting beliefs can also arise from personal experiences and trauma. Negative events, failures, or rejections can reinforce beliefs of unworthiness or incompetence. Traumatic experiences can deeply impact our self-image and create beliefs of fear, unworthiness, or powerlessness.

Exploring these experiences and their influence on our beliefs allows us to release their hold on us.

4. Internalized Messages and Self-Perception: Over time, we internalize the messages we receive and create a narrative about ourselves. This internal dialogue shapes our self-perception and influences our beliefs. Examining our internalized messages, such as self-criticism or self-doubt, helps us uncover the root causes of our limiting beliefs and understand how they contribute to our self-image.

5. Reflecting on Patterns and Triggers: Recognizing patterns and triggers associated with our limiting beliefs is crucial in examining their origins. Certain situations, relationships, or environments may consistently activate these beliefs. By reflecting on these patterns and triggers, we can identify the specific experiences or messages that initially instilled these beliefs within us.

6. Journaling and Self-Reflection: Journaling and self-reflection are powerful tools for exploring the origins of limiting beliefs. Writing down our thoughts, emotions, and memories allows us to gain clarity and insight into the events and experiences that have influenced our beliefs. Through journaling, we can uncover hidden connections and patterns that contribute to our self-perception.

7. Seeking Professional Support: Examining the origins of limiting beliefs can be a challenging and emotional process. Seeking support from therapists, counselors, or coaches who specialize in belief transformation can provide guidance and a safe space for exploration. These professionals can help navigate the deep-rooted beliefs and assist in releasing their hold on our self-image.

8. Releasing and Replacing Limiting Beliefs: Once we have examined the origins of our limiting beliefs, it is essential to release them and replace them with empowering

beliefs. This involves consciously challenging and reframing our thoughts, affirming our strengths and capabilities, and consciously choosing new narratives that align with our desired self-image.

Understanding the origins of limiting beliefs is a transformative process that allows us to release the grip of these beliefs and create a positive self-image. By exploring childhood experiences and conditioning, cultural and societal influences, personal experiences and trauma, internalized messages, reflecting on patterns and triggers, journaling, seeking professional support, and releasing and replacing limiting beliefs, we can rewrite our narrative and cultivate empowering beliefs that support our personal growth, success, and self-esteem.

Techniques for Reframing and Replacing Negative Beliefs with Empowering Ones

To cultivate confidence, belief, and self-esteem, it is essential to reframe and replace negative beliefs with empowering ones. Reframing involves shifting our perspective and finding alternative interpretations, while replacing involves consciously choosing new beliefs that support our growth and well-being.

1. Cognitive Restructuring: Cognitive restructuring is a powerful technique that involves challenging and replacing negative thoughts with more positive and rational ones. By identifying the negative belief, examining the evidence supporting or refuting it, and consciously choosing a more empowering perspective, we can reframe our thinking patterns and develop a more optimistic and supportive Mind-set.

2. Thought Stopping: Thought stopping is a technique used to interrupt and halt negative thought patterns. Whenever a negative belief arises, we can visualize a stop sign or say "stop" in our minds. This creates a

moment of pause, allowing us to consciously choose a different thought or belief that aligns with our desired self-image.

3. Thought Replacement: Thought replacement involves consciously replacing negative thoughts with positive and empowering ones. When we catch ourselves engaging in negative self-talk or beliefs, we can immediately counteract them with affirmations or statements that reflect our strengths, abilities, and potential. By consistently practicing thought replacement, we rewire our thinking patterns and reinforce empowering beliefs.
4. Visualizations and Mental Imagery: Visualizations and mental imagery are powerful tools for reframing and replacing negative beliefs. By vividly imagining ourselves succeeding, achieving our goals, and embodying qualities we desire, we create new neural pathways in our minds that support our positive self-image. Regularly engaging in positive visualizations strengthens our belief in ourselves and aligns our thoughts with our desired outcomes.
5. Empowering Self-Questioning: Challenging negative beliefs through empowering self-questioning is an effective technique for reframing our thoughts. By asking ourselves empowering questions such as, "What evidence contradicts this belief?" or "How can I interpret this situation in a more positive light?" we open ourselves up to new perspectives and possibilities. This helps us replace negative beliefs with more empowering and constructive ones.
6. Gathering Supporting Evidence: When faced with a negative belief, gathering supporting evidence can be an empowering practice. This involves actively seeking out examples, experiences, or feedback that contradicts the negative belief. By focusing on evidence that

supports our competence, strengths, and accomplishments, we build a reservoir of positive references that counteract the negative belief.

7. Positive Affirmations and Self-Talk: Positive affirmations and self-talk are instrumental in replacing negative beliefs with empowering ones. By consciously choosing and repeating positive statements about ourselves, our abilities, and our worth, we reprogram our subconscious mind and reinforce empowering beliefs. Regularly practicing positive self-talk builds self-confidence and nurtures a positive self-image.

8. Surrounding Yourself with Supportive Influences: The people we surround ourselves with have a significant impact on our beliefs and self-image. Surrounding ourselves with supportive and uplifting influences, such as positive-minded friends, mentors, or role models, reinforces empowering beliefs. Engaging in conversations and activities that uplift and inspire us helps to reframe negative beliefs and create a positive and supportive environment.

Reframing and replacing negative beliefs with empowering ones is a transformative process that cultivates confidence, belief, and self-esteem. By utilizing techniques such as cognitive restructuring, thought stopping, thought replacement, visualizations, empowering self-questioning, gathering supporting evidence, positive affirmations and self-talk, and surrounding ourselves with supportive influences, we can shift our Mind-set and develop a positive self-image. With consistent practice

5

Embracing Your Uniqueness: Celebrating Authenticity

Embracing your uniqueness is about fully accepting and celebrating your individuality, including your strengths, quirks, passions, and perspectives. Here are some ways to embrace your uniqueness:

1. Self-acceptance: Start by accepting yourself as you are, with all your strengths and imperfections. Embrace the idea that it's okay to be different and that your uniqueness is what makes you special. Emphasize self-love and self-compassion in your relationship with yourself.

2. Celebrate your strengths: Recognize and celebrate your unique strengths and talents. Identify the things you excel at or the qualities that make you stand out. Embrace and develop these strengths, as they contribute to your unique identity and can help you make a positive impact.

3. Embrace your quirks: Embrace the quirks and idiosyncrasies that make you different. Don't be afraid to show your true personality and let your authentic self shine. Remember that it's your unique traits that make you interesting and memorable.

4. Pursue your passions: Identify and pursue the activities, hobbies, or causes that genuinely inspire and energize you. Follow your passions and allow them to shape your life. Your unique interests and passions can bring fulfillment and a sense of purpose.

5. Value your perspectives: Recognize the value of your perspectives and opinions. Your unique experiences, beliefs, and insights can offer fresh and valuable perspectives to the world. Embrace your voice and share your thoughts with confidence.

6. Surround yourself with supportive people: Surround yourself with people who appreciate and celebrate your uniqueness. Seek out relationships with individuals who embrace diversity and value authenticity. Having a supportive network can boost your confidence in being yourself.

7. Challenge societal expectations: Be aware of societal expectations and norms that may pressure you to conform. Challenge the notion that there is a single "right" way to be or live. Create your own path and define success and happiness on your terms.

8. Practice self-expression: Find outlets for self-expression that resonate with you. This can include art, writing, music, dance, or any other creative form that allows you to express your unique thoughts and emotions. Use these outlets as vehicles to celebrate your authenticity.

9. Embrace growth and learning: Continuously seek opportunities for personal growth and learning. Be open to new experiences, perspectives, and ideas. Embracing growth allows you to expand your horizons and discover new aspects of your uniqueness.

10. Embody self-confidence: Embrace self-confidence by trusting in your abilities and the value you bring. Believe in yourself and your unique contributions. Embodying self-confidence allows you to navigate the world with authenticity and poise.

Remember that embracing your uniqueness is an ongoing journey. It may involve overcoming self-doubt and societal pressures. Be patient with yourself and practice self-acceptance and self-compassion along the way. Embracing your uniqueness allows you to live a more fulfilling and authentic life while inspiring others to do the same.

Embracing our uniqueness and celebrating authenticity is a powerful way to cultivate confidence, belief, and self-esteem. When we honor and express our true selves, we create a sense of fulfillment and genuine connection with others.

1. Understanding Authenticity: Authenticity is the state of being true to oneself, embracing our genuine thoughts, emotions, values, and beliefs. It involves aligning our actions with our inner truth and expressing ourselves without fear of judgment or rejection. Understanding and embracing authenticity is a vital step in nurturing our self-image and overall well-being.
2. Recognizing the Benefits of Authenticity: Embracing authenticity brings numerous benefits to our lives. It allows us to build genuine connections with others based on trust and mutual understanding. Living authentically enhances our self-confidence and self-esteem as we no longer have to hide or pretend to be someone we are not. It also fosters a sense of purpose and fulfillment, as we engage in activities and pursuits that resonate with our true selves.
3. Self-Reflection and Self-Awareness: To embrace our uniqueness and live authentically, self-reflection and self-awareness are key. Taking time to explore our values, passions, strengths, and aspirations helps us understand our authentic selves better. Engaging in practices such as journaling, meditation, or therapy can facilitate self-reflection and deepen our self-awareness.
4. Embracing Imperfections: Authenticity involves embracing our imperfections and recognizing that they are an inherent part of our uniqueness. By accepting and embracing our flaws, we free ourselves from the pressure of perfection and allow room for growth,

learning, and self-compassion. Embracing our imperfections also encourages others to embrace theirs, fostering a culture of acceptance and authenticity.

5. Expressing Your True Self: Living authentically means expressing our true selves in all areas of life. This includes our personal relationships, professional endeavors, and creative pursuits. By expressing our thoughts, emotions, and values authentically, we invite others to do the same, creating an environment of openness and genuine connection.
6. Setting Boundaries: Embracing authenticity requires setting boundaries to protect our true selves. Establishing clear boundaries helps us maintain our authenticity and prevents us from compromising our values or needs to please others. Setting boundaries allows us to honor ourselves and ensures that our actions and interactions align with our authentic selves.
7. Celebrating Uniqueness in Relationships: Authenticity in relationships involves embracing and celebrating the uniqueness of both ourselves and others. It requires open communication, vulnerability, and a willingness to accept and appreciate each other's differences. By celebrating the authenticity of others, we create a supportive and nurturing environment for everyone involved.
8. Embracing Authenticity in Career and Life Choices: Living authentically extends to our career and life choices. It involves aligning our professional paths and life decisions with our values, passions, and aspirations. By pursuing work and activities that resonate with our authentic selves, we experience a sense of fulfillment and purpose. Embracing authenticity in our career and life choices allows us to create a life that is true to who we are.

Embracing our uniqueness and celebrating authenticity is a transformative journey that cultivates confidence, belief, and self-esteem. By understanding authenticity, recognizing its benefits, engaging in self-reflection, embracing imperfections, expressing our true selves, setting boundaries, celebrating uniqueness in relationships, and embracing authenticity in career and life choices, we create a life that is in alignment with our true selves.

Honouring Your True Self

Honoring your true self is about living in alignment with your authentic values, desires, and beliefs. It involves embracing who you truly are and making choices that reflect your genuine identity. Here are some ways to honor your true self:

1. Self-reflection: Take time for self-reflection and introspection. Understand your values, passions, and what brings you joy and fulfillment. Connect with your inner thoughts and emotions to gain clarity about who you are at your core.
2. Embrace authenticity: Be true to yourself and express who you are without fear of judgment or rejection. Embrace your unique qualities, interests, and perspectives. Avoid trying to be someone you're not just to please others or fit societal expectations.
3. Set boundaries: Establish clear boundaries that protect your well-being and honor your values. Learn to say no to things that don't align with your true self, and prioritize activities and relationships that nourish and support your authentic identity.
4. Trust your intuition: Tune in to your intuition and inner guidance. Trust your instincts and listen to the voice within you. Your intuition can guide you towards choices and paths that resonate with your true self.

5. Practice self-care: Prioritize self-care activities that nurture your physical, emotional, and mental well-being. Engage in practices such as exercise, meditation, spending time in nature, or engaging in hobbies that bring you joy and relaxation. Taking care of yourself is a way of honoring and respecting your true self.

6. Surround yourself with supportive relationships: Cultivate relationships with people who accept and support you for who you are. Surround yourself with individuals who encourage your growth, share similar values, and appreciate your authentic self. Let go of toxic relationships that undermine your sense of self-worth.

7. Live in alignment with your values: Identify your core values and make choices that align with them. When your actions are congruent with your values, you feel a sense of integrity and fulfillment. Aligning your life with your values allows you to live in harmony with your true self.

8. Practice self-compassion: Be kind and compassionate towards yourself. Embrace your imperfections and treat yourself with love and understanding. Practice self-forgiveness and let go of self-judgment. Accept that you are a work in progress, and honor your true self by being gentle and patient with yourself.

9. Take risks and embrace growth: Step outside of your comfort zone and embrace opportunities for personal growth and self-discovery. Be open to new experiences, challenges, and learning opportunities. Honoring your true self means being willing to evolve and grow.

10. Live with authenticity and integrity: Be true to your word and act in alignment with your beliefs and values. Live with integrity by being honest and genuine in your interactions with others. When you live authentically and with integrity, you honor your true self and build a strong sense of self-respect.

Remember, honoring your true self is an ongoing journey. It requires self-awareness, self-acceptance, and a willingness to make choices that align with your authentic identity. Embrace the process, be patient with yourself, and celebrate the unique and beautiful person that you are.

Honouring your true self is a profound act of self-respect and self-love. It involves embracing your values, passions, needs, and desires, and living in alignment with them. When you honor your true self, you create a life that is authentic, fulfilling, and meaningful. The importance of honouring your true self, the challenges that may arise, and practical strategies for staying true to who you are.

1. Authenticity as a Foundation: Authenticity serves as a foundation for honoring your true self. It requires self-awareness and a deep understanding of your values, beliefs, and aspirations. By connecting with your authentic self, you gain clarity about who you are and what truly matters to you.

2. Embracing Personal Values: Your values are the guiding principles that shape your decisions and actions. Honoring your true self involves identifying and embracing your personal values. Reflect on what is most important to you in life, what principles you want to live by, and make choices that align with those values.

3. Listening to Your Inner Voice: Your inner voice, intuition, or gut feeling is a powerful compass guiding you toward your true self. Honoring your true self requires cultivating a connection with your inner voice and learning to listen to its wisdom. Pay attention to the signals your intuition sends you and trust yourself to make decisions that are in alignment with your true desires.

4. Saying No to External Expectations: One of the challenges in honoring your true self is dealing with external expectations and societal pressures. It is

important to recognize that you have the right to live life on your own terms. Say no to activities, relationships, or obligations that don't align with your true self. Set boundaries and prioritize your well-being.

5. Practicing Self-Expression: Self-expression is a powerful way to honor your truc self. Find creative outlets, hobbies, or activities that allow you to express your thoughts, emotions, and unique perspective. It can be through art, writing, music, dance, or any form of self-expression that resonates with you. Allow yourself the freedom to be authentic and genuine in your self-expression.

6. Cultivating Self-Compassion: Honouring your true self involves practicing self-compassion. Be kind and forgiving toward yourself as you navigate through life. Embrace your imperfections and learn from your mistakes. Treat yourself with the same love, care, and understanding that you would offer to a dear friend.

7. Surrounding Yourself with Supportive Relationships: Nurturing supportive relationships is essential in honouring your true self. Surround yourself with people who accept and celebrate you for who you are. Build a network of individuals who support your growth and encourage you to be authentic. Engage in meaningful conversations and connections that uplift and inspire you.

8. Continuous Self-Reflection: Honouring your true self is an on-going process of self-reflection and self-discovery. Set aside time for regular self-reflection to check in with yourself and assess whether you are living in alignment with your true self. Explore your passions, interests, and evolving desires. Adjust your path as needed to ensure you stay true to who you are.

Honouring your true self is a transformative journey that requires self-awareness, courage, and self-compassion. By embracing your values, listening to your inner voice, saying no to external expectations, practicing self-expression, cultivating self-compassion, nurturing supportive relationships, and engaging in continuous self-reflection, you create a life that honors and celebrates your true self. Remember, you deserve to live authentically and to embrace the unique qualities that make you who you are.

Overcoming the Fear of Judgment and Rejection

The fear of judgment and rejection can significantly hinder our ability to honor our true selves and live authentically. It holds us back from expressing our unique qualities, pursuing our passions, and embracing our individuality. Overcoming the fear of judgment and rejection can be a transformative process that allows you to live more authentically and confidently. Here are some strategies to help you overcome this fear:

1. Recognize the source of fear: Understand that the fear of judgment and rejection often stems from a desire for acceptance and a fear of not being enough. Recognizing the source of your fear can help you address it more effectively.

2. Challenge irrational beliefs: Question the beliefs and assumptions that contribute to your fear of judgment and rejection. Ask yourself if these beliefs are based on reality or if they are distorted perceptions. Challenge negative self-talk and replace it with more rational and empowering thoughts.

3. Shift your perspective: Reframe judgment and rejection as opportunities for growth and learning. Instead of viewing them as personal attacks, see them as experiences that can strengthen your resilience and character. Remember that everyone has different opinions, and not everyone's judgment holds truth or significance.

4. Focus on self-acceptance: Cultivate self-acceptance and self-compassion. Develop a positive relationship with yourself by acknowledging your worthiness and embracing your unique qualities. When you accept yourself, the opinions of others have less power to shake your confidence.
5. Surround yourself with supportive people: Seek out relationships with individuals who uplift and support you. Surrounding yourself with a supportive network of friends, family, or mentors can provide encouragement and a sense of belonging, making it easier to face potential judgment or rejection.
6. Practice vulnerability: Engage in acts of vulnerability by sharing your authentic self and expressing your true thoughts and emotions. Start small, gradually expanding your comfort zone. Vulnerability fosters deeper connections with others and can often lead to more positive responses than anticipated.
7. Focus on personal growth: Shift your focus from seeking approval from others to personal growth and self-improvement. Set goals, develop new skills, and engage in activities that align with your passions and values. The more you invest in your personal growth, the less validation you'll need from external sources.
8. Challenge the need for perfection: Understand that perfection is an unrealistic standard and striving for it can hold you back. Embrace your imperfections and recognize that making mistakes is a natural part of growth and learning. Allow yourself to be human and embrace the learning opportunities that come with failure.
9. Practice self-validation: Develop the habit of validating yourself rather than relying solely on external validation. Recognize your accomplishments, acknowledge your efforts, and celebrate your progress.

Internal validation allows you to build self-esteem and reduces the need for constant approval from others.

10. Seek professional support if needed: If the fear of judgment and rejection significantly impacts your daily life and well-being, consider seeking support from a therapist or counselor. They can provide guidance and help you work through deeper underlying issues.
11. Understanding the Fear: The fear of judgment and rejection often stems from a deep-seated need for acceptance and belonging. It may have roots in past experiences of criticism, rejection, or social pressure. By understanding the origins of this fear, we can begin to unravel its hold on us and take steps toward overcoming it.
12. Challenging Negative Beliefs: The fear of judgment and rejection is often fueled by negative beliefs about ourselves and what others may think of us. Challenge these beliefs by examining the evidence supporting them and considering alternative perspectives. Replace negative beliefs with empowering ones that affirm your worth and uniqueness.
13. Reframing Mistakes and Failure: Fear of judgment and rejection can intensify our fear of making mistakes or failing. Reframe your perspective on mistakes and failure as opportunities for growth and learning. Embrace a mind-set that recognizes that setbacks are a natural part of the journey toward success and self-improvement.
14. Cultivating Self-Confidence: Building self-confidence is crucial in overcoming the fear of judgment and rejection. Focus on developing your strengths, skills, and abilities. Celebrate your accomplishments and remind yourself of your past successes. Engage in positive self-talk and affirmations that reinforce your self-belief.

15. Gradual Exposure: Overcoming the fear of judgment and rejection requires gradually exposing yourself to situations that trigger these fears. Start with small steps that challenge your comfort zone. As you experience positive outcomes and realize that the fear is often exaggerated, your confidence will grow, and the fear will diminish.

16. Building a Support System: Surround yourself with a supportive network of friends, family, or mentors who accept and appreciate you for who you are. Seek out individuals who encourage your authenticity and provide a safe space for you to express yourself without fear of judgment or rejection. Their support can help boost your confidence and resilience.

17. Practicing Vulnerability: Vulnerability is a powerful antidote to the fear of judgment and rejection. Open up and share your authentic thoughts, feelings, and experiences with trusted individuals. By allowing yourself to be vulnerable, you create deeper connections and invite others to do the same. Embrace vulnerability as a strength, not a weakness.

18. Focusing on Self-Approval: Shift your focus from seeking external approval to cultivating self-approval. Recognize that your worth and validation come from within, not from others' opinions. Practice self-acceptance and self-compassion. Celebrate your unique qualities and embrace the fact that not everyone will understand or resonate with you—and that's okay.

Overcoming the fear of judgment and rejection is a liberating journey that allows us to embrace our authentic selves fully. By understanding the roots of this fear, challenging negative beliefs, reframing mistakes, cultivating self-confidence, gradually exposing ourselves to triggers, building a support system, practicing vulnerability, and focusing on self-approval, we can break free from the constraints of fear and live authentically. Remember, your uniqueness is a gift, and the world deserves to experience it.

Remember that overcoming the fear of judgment and rejection is a gradual process. Be patient with yourself and celebrate your progress along the way. As you embrace your authentic self and cultivate self-acceptance, the fear will gradually lose its power, and you will become more resilient and confident in the face of potential judgment or rejection.

6

Stepping Out of Your Comfort Zone: Expanding Your Confidence

Expanding your confidence is an empowering process that allows you to step into your full potential and achieve greater success in various areas of life. Here are some strategies to help you expand your confidence:

1. Set realistic goals: Set specific, achievable goals that align with your values and aspirations. Break them down into smaller, manageable steps, and celebrate each milestone you achieve. Accomplishing goals boosts your confidence and motivates you to take on bigger challenges.

2. Step out of your comfort zone: Challenge yourself to step outside of your comfort zone regularly. Take on new experiences, try new activities, and embrace opportunities for growth and learning. Each time you face and conquer a new challenge, your confidence expands.

3. Develop a growth Mind-set: Adopt a growth Mind-set, which means believing that your abilities and intelligence can be developed through dedication and effort. Embrace challenges as opportunities to learn and improve, rather than seeing setbacks as failures. Emphasize the power of learning and perseverance in building confidence.

4. Practice self-care: Take care of your physical, mental, and emotional well-being. Prioritize activities that

recharge and rejuvenate you. Engage in regular exercise, get enough sleep, eat nourishing foods, and practice relaxation techniques such as meditation or deep breathing. When you prioritize self-care, you feel better about yourself and have more confidence in your abilities.

5. Celebrate your strengths: Recognize and celebrate your unique strengths and talents. Identify what you excel at and the qualities that make you valuable. Embrace and develop these strengths, and remind yourself of them regularly. Focusing on your strengths builds confidence and provides a solid foundation for personal growth.
6. Build a support network: Surround yourself with supportive and encouraging individuals who believe in you and your abilities. Seek out mentors, friends, or colleagues who inspire and uplift you. Their positive feedback and support can boost your confidence and provide valuable guidance along your journey.
7. Practice self-compassion: Be kind and compassionate toward yourself. Embrace self-acceptance and forgive yourself for mistakes or setbacks. Treat yourself with understanding and patience, just as you would with a dear friend. Self-compassion allows you to build a positive relationship with yourself, which strengthens your confidence.
8. Learn from failure: Embrace failure as an opportunity to learn and grow. Instead of allowing failure to diminish your confidence, see it as a stepping stone toward success. Analyze what went wrong, extract the lessons, and adjust your approach. Every setback provides valuable insights and resilience-building experiences.
9. Take care of your appearance: While confidence comes from within, taking care of your appearance can

positively impact how you feel about yourself. Dress in a way that makes you feel good, practice good hygiene, and present yourself with confidence. When you feel comfortable and put-together, it can enhance your self-assurance.

10. Visualize success: Use visualization techniques to imagine yourself succeeding in challenging situations. Create vivid mental images of yourself confidently accomplishing your goals. Visualizing success helps build a positive Mind-set and reinforces your belief in your abilities.

Remember, expanding your confidence is a process that requires consistency and patience. Celebrate your successes, big and small, along the way. As you embrace new experiences, build supportive relationships, and prioritize self-care, your confidence will naturally expand, enabling you to reach new heights in all areas of your life.

Our comfort zone is a familiar and safe space where we feel secure and in control. However, true growth and expanded confidence lie beyond its boundaries. Stepping out of your comfort zone is a powerful way to challenge yourself, overcome self-imposed limitations, and cultivate a greater sense of confidence and belief in your abilities.

1. Understanding the Comfort Zone: The comfort zone is a psychological state where we feel at ease, with minimal stress or anxiety. While it provides a sense of security, staying within its boundaries limits personal growth and stifles our potential. Recognizing the comfort zone as a self-imposed limitation is the first step toward expanding it.

2. Embracing the Benefits of Discomfort: Stepping out of your comfort zone may feel uncomfortable or even intimidating at first, but it offers numerous benefits. By pushing your boundaries, you gain new experiences, skills, and perspectives. You build resilience and

adaptability, fostering personal growth and self-confidence. Embracing discomfort as a catalyst for growth is essential.

3. Setting Realistic Goals: Start by setting realistic and achievable goals that push you slightly outside your comfort zone. Break down larger goals into smaller, manageable steps. By setting clear objectives, you create a roadmap for expanding your comfort zone in a structured and manageable way.
4. Embracing a Growth Mind-set: Adopting a growth Mind-set is crucial when stepping out of your comfort zone. Embrace challenges as opportunities for learning and growth, rather than fearing failure or setbacks. See obstacles as chances to develop new skills and discover untapped potential within yourself.
5. Taking Calculated Risks: Stepping out of your comfort zone often involves taking risks. Assess the potential risks and rewards of a particular situation and make informed decisions. Understand that taking calculated risks is essential for personal and professional development. By embracing risks, you open doors to new possibilities and experiences.
6. Embracing Failure as Learning: Fear of failure is a common barrier to stepping out of your comfort zone. Embrace failure as a natural part of the learning process and an opportunity for growth. Learn from your mistakes, extract valuable lessons, and use them to refine your approach. Remember that failures do not define you—they are stepping stones on the path to success.
7. Seeking New Experiences: To expand your comfort zone, actively seek out new experiences. Engage in activities or pursue interests that are outside your usual scope. Join clubs, attend workshops, travel to unfamiliar

places, or try new hobbies. By exposing yourself to diverse experiences, you broaden your perspective and build confidence in navigating unfamiliar territory.

8. Cultivating Resiliencc: Stepping out of your comfort zone can be challenging, and setbacks may occur along the way. Cultivate resilience by maintaining a positive Mind-set, practicing self-care, and seeking support when needed. Surround yourself with a network of individuals who uplift and encourage you, providing guidance and motivation during difficult times.

Stepping out of your comfort zone is a transformative journey that expands your confidence and belief in your abilities. By recognizing the limitations of the comfort zone, embracing discomfort as a catalyst for growth, setting realistic goals, adopting a growth Mind-set, taking calculated risks, embracing failure as learning, seeking new experiences, and cultivating resilience, you embark on a path of personal growth and expanded confidence. Remember, your potential lies just beyond the boundaries of your comfort zone—embrace the challenge and watch yourself soar.

The Power of Stretching Your Boundaries

Within each of us lie untapped potential and unexplored possibilities. Stretching your boundaries is the process of pushing past your limitations and venturing into new territories, both personally and professionally. It is through this stretching that you can unlock hidden strengths, broaden your horizons, and discover the depth of your capabilities.

Stretching your boundaries is a powerful practice that can lead to personal growth, self-discovery, and expanded possibilities. When you stretch your boundaries, you step outside of your comfort zone and challenge yourself to go beyond what feels familiar or safe. Here are some reasons why stretching your boundaries is powerful:

1. Personal growth: Stretching your boundaries pushes you to grow and develop as an individual. By venturing into new experiences, taking on challenges, and facing fears, you expand your skills, knowledge, and perspectives. This process fosters personal development and helps you discover your strengths and capabilities.

2. Overcoming limitations: Stretching your boundaries allows you to break free from self-imposed limitations or limiting beliefs. It helps you challenge the idea of what you thought you were capable of and expands your sense of what is possible. By pushing past your comfort zone, you realize that you are capable of more than you previously believed.

3. Building resilience: Stepping outside of your comfort zone and facing challenges helps you build resilience. It teaches you to navigate uncertainty, adapt to new situations, and bounce back from setbacks. This resilience not only strengthens your confidence but also equips you with the tools to overcome future obstacles.

4. Expanded perspective: When you stretch your boundaries, you expose yourself to new ideas, cultures, and ways of thinking. This exposure broadens your perspective and helps you see the world from different angles. It enhances your empathy, understanding, and tolerance for diversity, fostering personal growth and enriching your relationships.

5. Increased self-confidence: Successfully stretching your boundaries boosts your self-confidence. Each time you face a challenge and overcome it, you gain confidence in your abilities and become more self-assured. This newfound confidence spills over into other areas of your life, empowering you to take on even greater challenges.

6. Discovering new passions and interests: Stretching your boundaries opens doors to new experiences, passions,

and interests. It allows you to explore different aspects of life and discover hidden talents or passions you may not have known existed. By trying new things, you may find activities or paths that bring you immense joy and fulfillment.

7. Breaking through fears: Stretching your boundaries requires confronting fears and stepping into the unknown. By facing your fears head-on, you diminish their power over you and gain a sense of empowerment. Breaking through fears expands your comfort zone and frees you to pursue your goals and dreams with greater courage.

8. Enhanced creativity and problem-solving skills: Stretching your boundaries stimulates your creativity and problem-solving skills. When you expose yourself to new experiences and challenges, you are forced to think outside the box and find innovative solutions. This creativity can permeate into other areas of your life, enhancing your overall problem-solving abilities.

9. Empowerment and self-empowerment: Stretching your boundaries empowers you to take control of your life and make conscious choices. It shifts your Mind-set from being passive to actively seeking growth and opportunities. By pushing your boundaries, you become an active participant in shaping your own life, leading to a greater sense of empowerment and fulfillment.

10. Living a fulfilling and meaningful life: By stretching your boundaries, you create a life that is rich with experiences, growth, and fulfillment. Embracing new challenges and opportunities allows you to live a life of purpose and meaning. It opens doors to possibilities and helps you create a life that aligns with your values and passions.

11. Embracing Growth and Development: Stretching your boundaries starts with embracing a Mind-set of growth and development. Recognize that you're potential for growth is limitless and that you can continuously learn and improve. Embrace the idea that stepping outside your comfort zone is necessary for progress and personal fulfilment.
12. Challenging Self-Limiting Beliefs: Self-limiting beliefs often hold us back from exploring new possibilities and stretching our boundaries. Identify and challenge these beliefs by examining the evidence supporting them. Replace them with empowering beliefs that encourage you to reach beyond what you thought was possible.
13. Setting Stretch Goals: Setting stretch goals involves aiming for achievements that lie just beyond your current capabilities. These goals should be challenging but still attainable with effort and dedication. By setting stretch goals, you motivate yourself to go beyond your comfort zone and tap into your untapped potential.
14. Embracing Discomfort: Stretching your boundaries requires embracing discomfort. Understand that growth and expansion often involve stepping into the unknown and facing unfamiliar situations. Embrace the discomfort as a sign that you are pushing yourself and growing as an individual.
15. Taking Calculated Risks: Stretching your boundaries involves taking calculated risks. Assess the potential risks and rewards of a particular endeavor and make informed decisions. Understand that risks are opportunities for growth and view failures as valuable learning experiences that contribute to your overall development.
16. Seeking New Perspectives: Stretching your boundaries involves seeking new perspectives and exploring diverse viewpoints. Engage with people from different

backgrounds, cultures, and fields of expertise. This exposure to varied perspectives broadens your understanding and challenges your preconceived notions, expanding your mental boundaries.

17. Stepping Into Unfamiliar Territory: Stretching your boundaries often means venturing into unfamiliar territory. Be open to trying new experiences, whether it's taking on a new role at work, learning a new skill, or engaging in activities outside your comfort zone. Embrace the opportunity to grow, adapt, and discover hidden strengths within yourself.

18. Celebrating Growth and Progress: As you stretch your boundaries and venture into new realms, celebrate your growth and progress along the way. Acknowledge and appreciate the courage it takes to step outside your comfort zone. Celebrate small victories and milestones, as they reinforce your belief in your ability to stretch further.

Stretching your boundaries is a transformative journey that leads to personal growth, increased confidence, and expanded possibilities. By embracing growth, challenging self-limiting beliefs, setting stretch goals, embracing discomfort, taking calculated risks, seeking new perspectives, stepping into unfamiliar territory, and celebrating growth and progress, you open yourself up to a world of opportunities and potential. Remember, by stretching your boundaries, you unlock the power within you to create a more fulfilling and extraordinary life.

Remember, stretching your boundaries doesn't mean constantly living outside of your comfort zone. It means periodically challenging yourself to step beyond what feels familiar or safe. Start with small steps and gradually push your boundaries further. Embrace the discomfort that comes with growth, and you will unlock new levels of personal development and empowerment.

Setting and Achieving Goals to Build Confidence

Setting and achieving goals is a powerful way to build confidence and create a sense of accomplishment. By defining clear objectives and taking consistent action towards them, you can develop a strong belief in your abilities and witness tangible progress.

Setting and achieving goals is a powerful way to build confidence and propel yourself towards success. When you set clear and meaningful goals, you create a roadmap for personal growth and accomplishment. Here are some strategies for setting and achieving goals to build confidence:

1. Define your goals: Clearly define what you want to achieve. Make your goals specific, measurable, attainable, relevant, and time-bound (SMART). This clarity provides a clear direction and focus for your efforts.
2. Break them down: Break your goals into smaller, manageable steps. This makes them less overwhelming and allows you to track your progress more effectively. Each small achievement builds confidence and motivates you to keep moving forward.
3. Set realistic yet challenging goals: Ensure your goals are realistic and achievable, but also challenge you to step outside of your comfort zone. Pushing yourself beyond what feels comfortable fosters personal growth and builds confidence as you overcome obstacles and stretch your capabilities.
4. Create an action plan: Outline the specific actions you need to take to achieve your goals. Break them down into actionable tasks and set deadlines for each step. Having a plan helps you stay organized and focused, increasing your chances of success.

5. Visualize success: Visualize yourself achieving your goals and experiencing the positive outcomes. Create vivid mental images of your success and imagine how it will feel. Visualization reinforces your belief in your abilities and motivates you to take action.
6. Monitor and celebrate progress: Regularly track your progress towards your goals. Celebrate each milestone and acknowledge your achievements along the way. Recognizing your progress boosts your confidence and fuels your motivation to keep going.
7. Embrace setbacks as learning opportunities: Setbacks are a natural part of the goal-setting process. Instead of letting them discourage you, see them as valuable learning experiences. Analyze what went wrong, adjust your approach, and use setbacks as opportunities to grow and improve.
8. Seek support: Surround yourself with supportive individuals who believe in your abilities and goals. Share your goals with trusted friends, family, or mentors who can offer guidance, encouragement, and accountability. Their support can bolster your confidence and provide valuable insights.
9. Practice self-discipline and consistency: Building confidence through goal achievement requires discipline and consistency. Stay committed to your goals, even when faced with challenges or distractions. Develop daily habits and routines that align with your goals, and prioritize consistent action.
10. Reflect and learn from your achievements: Take time to reflect on your achievements and the lessons learned along the way. Recognize the growth you've experienced and the skills you've developed. This reflection reinforces your confidence and prepares you for future goals.

11. The Role of Goals in Confidence Building: Goals provide direction and purpose, giving you something to strive for and measure your progress against. When you set and achieve goals, you prove to yourself that you are capable of success, boosting your self-confidence. Goals also help you focus your efforts and provide a sense of fulfillment as you make progress towards your desired outcomes.

12. Setting SMART Goals: Effective goal-setting involves creating goals that are SMART: Specific, Measurable, Attainable, Relevant, and Time-bound. Specific goals clearly define what you want to achieve, while measurable goals have quantifiable criteria to track progress. Ensure your goals are attainable, challenging enough to stretch you but realistic enough to be within your reach. Make sure your goals align with your values and aspirations, giving them relevance. Finally, set a specific timeframe for achieving your goals to create a sense of urgency and accountability.

13. Breaking Down Goals into Actionable Steps: Large goals can feel overwhelming, leading to a lack of confidence and motivation. Break down your goals into smaller, actionable steps that are more manageable and less intimidating. Each step becomes a milestone that propels you forward, building momentum and confidence as you achieve them one by one.

14. Visualizing Success: Visualization is a powerful technique for building confidence and achieving goals. Take time to vividly imagine yourself successfully accomplishing your goals. Visualize the process, the challenges you overcome, and the emotions you will experience upon achieving them. This mental rehearsal primes your mind for success, boosting your confidence and motivation.

15. Developing a Plan and Tracking Progress: Create a detailed plan that outlines the specific actions you need to take to achieve your goals. Break it down into actionable tasks with deadlines. Regularly review and update your plan as needed. Track your progress along the way, celebrating milestones and adjusting your approach if necessary. The act of tracking progress keeps you accountable and provides a sense of achievement as you see your goals come to fruition.
16. Embracing a Growth Mind-set: Adopting a growth Mind-set is essential for building confidence and achieving goals. Embrace challenges and setbacks as opportunities for learning and growth. View obstacles as temporary roadblocks that can be overcome with effort and persistence. Believe in your capacity to develop new skills and abilities through dedication and practice.
17. Celebrating Achievements: Celebrate your achievements, no matter how big or small. Acknowledge and reward yourself for reaching milestones and successfully accomplishing your goals. Celebrations reinforce positive behavior and create a sense of satisfaction, further boosting your confidence and motivation.
18. Learning from Setbacks: Setbacks are a natural part of the goal achievement process. Instead of letting them discourage you, view setbacks as valuable learning experiences. Analyze what went wrong, adjust your approach if needed, and use the lessons learned to propel yourself forward. The ability to bounce back from setbacks with resilience and determination strengthens your confidence and increases your chances of future success.

Setting and achieving goals is a powerful tool for building confidence and fostering personal growth. By setting SMART goals, breaking them down into actionable steps, visualizing success, developing a plan, tracking progress, embracing a growth Mind-set, celebrating achievements, and learning from setbacks, you create a roadmap for success and boost your confidence along the way.

Remember, building confidence through goal achievement is a journey. Embrace the process, stay resilient in the face of challenges, and celebrate your progress. With each goal you set and achieve, you build a stronger belief in your abilities and cultivate a sense of self-assurance that extends beyond specific accomplishments.

7

Mastering Self-Presentation: Effective Communication and Body Language

Mastering self-presentation is an important skill that can significantly impact your personal and professional life. It involves presenting yourself in a confident, authentic, and effective manner to make a positive impression on others. Here are some strategies to help you master self-presentation:

1. Know your audience: Understand the context and the people you will be interacting with. Consider their expectations, values, and interests. Adapting your self-presentation to suit your audience can help you establish rapport and connect more effectively.
2. Project confidence: Confidence is key to making a strong self-presentation. Pay attention to your body language, maintain good posture, make eye contact, and speak clearly and assertively. Confidence in your abilities and ideas will inspire confidence in others.
3. Dress appropriately: Dress in a way that aligns with the occasion and the expectations of the setting. Pay attention to grooming, choose attire that makes you feel comfortable and confident, and ensure it reflects your personal style and professionalism.
4. Authenticity: Be true to yourself and present an authentic version of who you are. Avoid trying to be someone you're not or pretending to have qualities or experiences you don't possess. Authenticity builds trust and allows others to connect with you on a genuine level.

5. Effective communication: Develop strong communication skills to effectively express your thoughts, ideas, and emotions. Listen actively, ask thoughtful questions, and engage in meaningful conversations. Tailor your communication style to the situation and be mindful of non-verbal cues such as facial expressions and body language.
6. Highlight your strengths: Identify and emphasize your unique strengths and qualities. Understand what sets you apart and communicate these attributes confidently. Showcase your accomplishments and experiences that demonstrate your expertise and capabilities.
7. Preparation: Prepare in advance for situations where you need to present yourself, such as interviews, meetings, or presentations. Research the topic or organization, anticipate potential questions or objections, and practice your responses. Preparation increases your confidence and helps you deliver your message effectively.
8. Active listening: Actively listen to others and show genuine interest in what they have to say. Give them your full attention, validate their perspectives, and respond thoughtfully. Active listening demonstrates respect, fosters meaningful connections, and helps you adapt your self-presentation to meet the needs of the situation.
9. Positive body language: Pay attention to your body language as it can significantly impact how others perceive you. Maintain open and welcoming gestures, avoid crossing your arms or appearing closed off, and use appropriate facial expressions to convey interest and enthusiasm.
10. Continuous improvement: Regularly seek feedback from trusted individuals to improve your self-

presentation skills. Reflect on your interactions and learn from each experience. Seek opportunities to develop your communication, networking, and interpersonal skills through courses, workshops, or practice sessions.

Remember, mastering self-presentation is an ongoing process that requires self-awareness, practice, and adaptation. Be open to feedback, stay true to yourself, and continuously strive to improve your skills. By presenting yourself confidently, authentically, and effectively, you can make a positive and lasting impression on others and create meaningful connections in various aspects of your life.

Effective Communication

Effective communication is a crucial skill that impacts every aspect of our lives, from personal relationships to professional success. It involves the ability to express your thoughts, ideas, and feelings clearly and to listen actively and empathetically to others. Here are some key elements of effective communication:

1. Clear and concise expression: Communicate your thoughts and ideas in a clear and concise manner. Use simple and straightforward language, organize your thoughts logically, and avoid unnecessary jargon or complex terms. Be mindful of the context and adjust your communication style accordingly.
2. Active listening: Actively listen to others when they speak. Give your full attention, maintain eye contact, and show genuine interest. Avoid interrupting or formulating responses before the person has finished speaking. Paraphrase and summarize their points to ensure understanding and to show that you are engaged in the conversation.
3. Non-verbal communication: Pay attention to non-verbal cues such as body language, facial expressions, and tone

of voice. Align your non-verbal communication with your verbal message to ensure consistency. Be aware of your own non-verbal signals and interpret those of others to enhance understanding and connection.

4. Empathy and understanding: Cultivate empathy and strive to understand others' perspectives and feelings. Put yourself in their shoes and listen with an open mind. Show empathy by validating their emotions and experiences. This fosters trust, mutual respect, and effective communication.

5. Use of appropriate feedback: Provide constructive feedback that is specific, actionable, and respectful. Focus on the behavior or situation rather than attacking the person. Be mindful of timing and delivery to ensure your feedback is well-received and can contribute to growth and improvement.

6. Adaptability: Adapt your communication style to different situations and individuals. Recognize that people have diverse communication preferences and adjust your approach accordingly. Be sensitive to cultural differences and strive to communicate in a way that is inclusive and respectful.

7. Clarity in written communication: When communicating in writing, ensure your message is clear and well-structured. Use proper grammar, spelling, and punctuation. Organize your thoughts logically and use formatting (such as headings and bullet points) to enhance readability. Proofread your writing to avoid misunderstandings.

8. Respectful and constructive dialogue: Engage in respectful dialogue, even when there are disagreements. Listen to different perspectives and avoid personal attacks or derogatory language. Foster an environment where everyone feels comfortable expressing their opinions and ideas.

9. Open-mindedness: Be open to different ideas and perspectives. Avoid jumping to conclusions or making assumptions. Be willing to consider alternative viewpoints and be open to changing your own perspective based on new information or insights.

10. Practice self-awareness: Develop self-awareness about your own communication style and patterns. Reflect on how your communication may impact others and seek feedback to identify areas for improvement. Continuously work on refining your communication skills through practice and learning.

Remember, effective communication is a lifelong learning process. It requires active engagement, openness, and a commitment to improving your skills. By practicing effective communication, you can build stronger relationships, resolve conflicts, and achieve greater success in various aspects of your life.

Body Language

Body language refers to the non-verbal cues and signals that we use to communicate our thoughts, emotions, and intentions. It includes facial expressions, gestures, posture, eye contact, and other physical movements. Body language plays a significant role in communication and can convey messages even without saying a word. Here are some key aspects of body language:

1. Facial expressions: Our facial expressions can reveal a range of emotions, such as happiness, sadness, anger, surprise, or fear. Smiling, raising an eyebrow, furrowing the brow, or frowning are examples of facial expressions that can convey different feelings and attitudes.

2. Gestures: Gestures are hand movements that accompany our speech and add meaning to our words. They can include pointing, waving, thumbs-up, thumbs-down, and various hand motions. Gestures can

help emphasize key points, convey emotions, or clarify intentions.

3. Posture and body orientation: The way we hold ourselves and position our bodies sends signals about our confidence, attentiveness, and openness. Standing or sitting upright with an open posture (arms uncrossed, legs not crossed) conveys confidence and approachability. Leaning in can show interest and engagement in a conversation.

4. Eye contact: Eye contact is a powerful form of non-verbal communication. It indicates attentiveness, interest, and sincerity. Maintaining appropriate eye contact demonstrates respect and engagement in a conversation. However, cultural norms and personal preferences can influence eye contact patterns.

5. Proximity: The distance we keep between ourselves and others, known as personal space, can communicate our comfort level and relationship dynamics. Different cultures and contexts have varying norms regarding personal space, so it's important to be aware of and respect these boundaries.

6. Touch: Touch can communicate a range of emotions and messages. A handshake, hug, pat on the back, or gentle touch on the arm can convey warmth, connection, or support. However, it's crucial to respect personal boundaries and cultural norms related to touch.

7. Mirroring: Mirroring refers to subconsciously imitating or reflecting the body language of the person you are interacting with. It can occur through similar gestures, posture, or speech patterns. Mirroring can foster a sense of rapport and connection between individuals.

8. Microexpressions: Microexpressions are brief facial expressions that reveal true emotions, often lasting for only a fraction of a second. They can provide insights

into a person's genuine feelings, even when they are trying to conceal them.

9. Congruence: Congruence in body language means aligning your verbal and non-verbal communication. When your words, tone of voice, facial expressions, and body language are in harmony, it enhances the credibility and clarity of your message.
10. Context and cultural considerations: It's important to recognize that body language can be influenced by cultural norms and individual differences. Gestures, facial expressions, and physical proximity can have different meanings in different cultures. Being aware of cultural variations and adapting accordingly is crucial for effective communication.

Understanding and interpreting body language can help you better understand others and be more aware of the signals you are sending. It is important to consider body language in conjunction with other verbal and contextual cues to gain a more accurate understanding of communication dynamics.

Self-presentation plays a vital role in how others perceive us and how we perceive ourselves. Effective communication and body language are essential components of self-presentation, influencing how confident, credible, and assertive we appear to others.

1. The Power of Effective Communication: Effective communication is crucial for conveying your thoughts, ideas, and emotions clearly and confidently. It involves both verbal and non-verbal communication. When you communicate effectively, you build rapport, foster understanding, and create meaningful connections with others. It also boosts your self-confidence as you express yourself authentically and assertively.
2. Active Listening: Active listening is a fundamental aspect of effective communication. It involves fully

engaging with the speaker, paying attention to their words, non-verbal cues, and underlying emotions. Practice active listening by maintaining eye contact, nodding to show understanding, and paraphrasing to confirm comprehension. This demonstrates respect, empathy, and enhances the quality of your interactions.

3. Clarity and Conciseness: Communicating with clarity and conciseness enhances your self-presentation. Express your thoughts in a clear and straightforward manner, using language that is appropriate for your audience. Avoid unnecessary jargon or complicated explanations. Focus on being concise while conveying your message effectively.
4. Assertive Communication: Assertive communication is a balance between being respectful of others' perspectives and expressing your own needs and opinions confidently. It involves using clear, direct language, maintaining appropriate body language, and expressing your thoughts and feelings without aggression or passivity. Practicing assertive communication builds confidence and fosters healthy relationships.
5. Non-Verbal Communication and Body Language: Non-verbal communication, including body language, plays a significant role in self-presentation. Pay attention to your body posture, gestures, facial expressions, and eye contact when interacting with others. Maintain an open and confident posture, make appropriate gestures to support your message, and maintain good eye contact to demonstrate attentiveness and confidence.
6. Power of Voice and Tone: Your voice and tone greatly influence how your message is received. Speak with a clear and confident voice, modulating your tone to convey your message effectively. Avoid speaking too softly or too loudly, as it may undermine your self-assurance. Practice speaking at a moderate pace, using

emphasis and pauses strategically to highlight important points.

7. Empathy and Emotional Intelligence: Developing empathy and emotional intelligence allows you to understand and connect with others on a deeper level. Show genuine interest in others' perspectives, validate their emotions, and respond empathetically. Cultivating emotional intelligence enhances your ability to communicate effectively and build positive relationships, ultimately boosting your self-confidence.
8. Continuous Improvement and Feedback: Self-presentation is a skill that can be continuously refined and improved. Seek feedback from trusted individuals to gain insights into your communication style and areas for growth. Actively work on addressing any areas of improvement, whether it's refining your body language, enhancing your vocal delivery, or developing stronger listening skills.

Mastering self-presentation through effective communication and body language is a transformative skill that enhances your confidence, credibility, and interpersonal connections. By practicing active listening, communicating with clarity and conciseness, embracing assertive communication, paying attention to non-verbal cues, leveraging the power of voice and tone, developing empathy and emotional intelligence, and seeking continuous improvement through feedback, you can elevate your self-presentation to new heights. Remember, effective self-presentation not only influences how others perceive you but also how you perceive yourself, allowing you to confidently express your true self and make a positive

Developing Confident Verbal and Non-verbal Communication Skills

Developing confident verbal and non-verbal communication skills is essential for expressing yourself effectively, building strong relationships, and navigating various social and professional situations. Here are some tips to help you enhance both aspects of your communication:

Verbal Communication Skills

Verbal communication skills are crucial for effective interpersonal interactions, presentations, public speaking, and conveying information clearly and persuasively. Here are some key aspects of verbal communication skills:

1. Clarity: Speak clearly and enunciate your words to ensure that your message is easily understood. Use appropriate language and vocabulary for your audience, avoiding jargon or complex terms that may cause confusion.

2. Tone and pitch: Pay attention to the tone and pitch of your voice. Varying your tone can add emphasis, convey different emotions, and keep your audience engaged. Use an appropriate volume and avoid speaking too softly or loudly.

3. Active listening: Effective verbal communication involves not only speaking but also actively listening to others. Give your full attention to the speaker, maintain eye contact, and respond appropriately to show that you are engaged and understanding their message.

4. Empathy and emotional intelligence: Show empathy by understanding and acknowledging the emotions and perspectives of others. Use words and phrases that convey empathy and support, such as "I understand," "I hear you," or "That must be challenging." Being emotionally intelligent allows you to respond appropriately to the emotions of others.

5. Structure and organization: Organize your thoughts and ideas in a logical manner when presenting information or speaking in public. Use a clear

introduction, main points, and a concise conclusion to help your audience follow your message easily.

6. Use of examples and anecdotes: Illustrate your points with relevant examples and anecdotes to make your message more relatable and engaging. Real-life examples can help your audience better understand and remember the information you are conveying.
7. Adaptability: Adapt your communication style to suit different audiences and situations. Consider the context, cultural norms, and the level of familiarity with the topic. Adjusting your language, tone, and level of formality can enhance understanding and connection.
8. Confidence and assertiveness: Project confidence and assertiveness when speaking. Believe in the value of your message and express it with conviction. Use confident body language, maintain good posture, and avoid excessive use of fillers like "um" or "uh."
9. Active engagement: Encourage active engagement from your audience by asking questions, soliciting feedback, or inviting participation. This fosters interaction, keeps the conversation dynamic, and shows that you value the input of others.
10. Continuous improvement: Seek opportunities to enhance your verbal communication skills through practice, feedback, and learning. Practice speaking in various settings, seek constructive feedback from trusted individuals, and take courses or workshops to develop specific areas of improvement.

Remember, effective verbal communication is not just about what you say but also how you say it. By honing your verbal communication skills, you can convey your thoughts and ideas more effectively, build rapport with others, and achieve better outcomes in your personal and professional interactions.

Non-Verbal Communication Skills

Non-verbal communication skills play a vital role in conveying messages, establishing rapport, and understanding others beyond the words they speak. Here are some key aspects of non-verbal communication skills:

1. Body language: Pay attention to your body posture, gestures, and movements. Use an open and relaxed posture to appear approachable and confident. Avoid crossed arms or defensive postures that may create barriers between you and others.

2. Facial expressions: Your facial expressions can convey a wealth of information. Use appropriate facial expressions to match the emotions and messages you want to communicate. Smiling, raising eyebrows, and maintaining a relaxed and engaged facial expression can help create a positive and receptive atmosphere.

3. Eye contact: Establish and maintain appropriate eye contact with others. It shows interest, attentiveness, and respect. However, cultural norms may vary, so be aware of different expectations regarding eye contact in different contexts.

4. Hand gestures: Use natural and purposeful hand gestures to emphasize and illustrate your points. Avoid excessive or distracting hand movements that can take away from your message. Use gestures that are congruent with your words to enhance understanding.

5. Tone of voice: Your tone of voice can convey emotions and attitudes. Vary your tone to reflect the message you want to convey, whether it's excitement, concern, or empathy. Use appropriate volume and avoid speaking too softly or loudly.

6. Proximity and personal space: Be aware of personal space and respect the comfort zones of others. Adjust

your proximity to others based on cultural norms and the nature of your relationship. Invading personal space can make others feel uncomfortable or threatened.

7. Mirroring and matching: Subtly mirror or match the body language of the person you are communicating with to establish rapport and connection. This can involve matching their posture, gestures, or facial expressions. However, be mindful of doing it naturally and respectfully, without mimicking or imitating excessively.
8. Microexpressions: Pay attention to microexpressions, which are fleeting facial expressions that reveal true emotions. These quick expressions can provide valuable insights into someone's genuine feelings, even if they are trying to conceal them.
9. Listening cues: Non-verbal cues can indicate your active listening and engagement. Nodding, maintaining eye contact, and using appropriate facial expressions can show that you are attentively listening and understanding the speaker's message.
10. Cultural sensitivity: Recognize that non-verbal communication cues can vary across cultures. Different cultures may have different meanings associated with body language, gestures, and personal space. Educate yourself about cultural differences to avoid misunderstandings and demonstrate respect.

Developing strong non-verbal communication skills involves self-awareness, observation, and practice. By understanding and effectively using non-verbal cues, you can enhance your communication, build stronger relationships, and improve your overall understanding of others.

Developing confidence through both verbal and non-verbal communication skills is crucial for several reasons:

1. Effective expression: When you have strong verbal and non-verbal communication skills, you can express your thoughts, ideas, and feelings clearly and confidently. This allows you to engage with others in a more impactful and persuasive manner.
2. Building rapport: Confident communication skills help in establishing rapport and building positive relationships with others. When you appear confident in your verbal and non-verbal cues, it encourages trust and openness, making others more receptive to your messages.
3. Influence and persuasion: Confidence in your communication skills allows you to effectively influence and persuade others. By conveying your thoughts and ideas confidently, using persuasive language, and employing strong non-verbal cues, you can inspire others to take action or adopt your viewpoint.
4. Assertiveness: Confidence in communication helps you assert yourself in a respectful and self-assured manner. It enables you to express your needs, opinions, and boundaries clearly and effectively, leading to more productive interactions and healthier relationships.
5. Public speaking and presentations: Verbal and non-verbal confidence are particularly crucial in public speaking and presentations. When you are confident in your delivery, maintain strong eye contact, use appropriate gestures, and project a confident tone of voice, you captivate your audience and enhance your message's impact.
6. Professional success: Confidence in communication is highly valued in the workplace. It allows you to participate actively in meetings, contribute ideas, and engage in effective collaborations. Confident communication skills can also help in job interviews, networking, and career advancement opportunities.

7. Self-expression and self-esteem: Developing confidence in your communication skills enables you to express yourself authentically and assert your identity. This enhances your self-esteem and self-worth, leading to a positive self-image and greater overall confidence in various areas of life.
8. Conflict resolution: Confidence in communication is vital for effectively navigating conflicts and resolving issues. When you express yourself confidently, it encourages open dialogue, active listening, and constructive problem-solving, leading to more positive outcomes in conflict resolution.
9. Overcoming fear and anxiety: Building confidence in communication helps overcome fear and anxiety associated with speaking or expressing oneself in public or challenging situations. As you develop and refine your skills, your confidence grows, allowing you to face communication challenges with greater ease and resilience.
10. Overall personal growth: Developing confidence in verbal and non-verbal communication skills is a significant aspect of personal growth. It enables you to express yourself authentically, connect with others, and navigate social interactions with ease. Confidence in communication contributes to a sense of empowerment, fulfillment, and personal development.

By consciously working on developing your verbal and non-verbal communication skills, you can enhance your confidence and positively impact various areas of your personal and professional life. Remember, developing confident verbal and non-verbal communication skills takes practice and self-awareness. Pay attention to how you communicate, seek feedback from others, and be open to continuous improvement. By honing these skills, you will convey confidence, connect more effectively with others, and enhance your overall communication abilities.

Enhancing Body Language and Presence

Body language and presence are powerful tools that contribute to how others perceive us and how we feel about ourselves. They play a crucial role in building confidence, establishing credibility, and making a lasting impression.

1. Posture and Alignment: Your posture is a key element of body language that conveys confidence and presence. Stand tall with your shoulders back, head held high, and spine aligned. Avoid slouching or crossing your arms, as these gestures can make you appear closed off or disengaged. Maintaining good posture not only signals confidence to others but also helps you feel more self-assured.

2. Eye Contact: Eye contact is a powerful non-verbal communication tool that establishes connection and engagement. Maintain consistent eye contact when interacting with others, as it shows attentiveness and confidence. However, be mindful of cultural norms and individual comfort levels, as excessive or prolonged eye contact may come across as intimidating. Strike a balance that reflects respect and interest.

3. Facial Expressions: Your facial expressions can convey a range of emotions and greatly influence how others perceive you. Practice maintaining a pleasant and approachable expression, with a genuine smile when appropriate. Be mindful of any unconscious facial expressions that may convey tension, anxiety, or disinterest. Paying attention to your facial expressions allows you to project warmth and confidence.

4. Gestures and Body Movements: Conscious use of gestures and body movements can enhance your presence and reinforce your message. Use natural and purposeful gestures to emphasize key points or to convey enthusiasm and passion. Avoid fidgeting or

excessive movements that may detract from your message. Practice a balance of controlled and expressive movements that complement your communication.

5. Vocal Presence: Your voice is an essential component of presence and effective communication. Develop vocal presence by speaking clearly and with confidence. Pay attention to the tone, volume, and pace of your speech. Practice varying your voice to add emphasis, modulate your pitch, and use pauses effectively. A strong and well-controlled voice enhances your presence and commands attention.

6. Body Language Alignment: Aligning your body language with your verbal communication is crucial for conveying authenticity and credibility. Ensure that your words, gestures, and facial expressions align with the message you are conveying. Incongruence between verbal and non-verbal cues can create confusion and undermine your presence. Practice maintaining consistency between your words and body language.

7. Mindfulness and Present Moment Awareness: Enhancing your body language and presence requires being present in the moment. Cultivate mindfulness by focusing on your physical sensations, breath, and surroundings. Being fully present allows you to respond authentically and engage with others in a meaningful way. Practice mindfulness to stay connected to the present moment and amplifies your presence.

8. Confidence and Self-Belief: Ultimately, enhancing body language and presence is rooted in cultivating confidence and self-belief. Develop self-confidence through self-acceptance, positive self-talk, and embracing your strengths. Believe in your abilities and the value you bring to interactions. As your confidence grows, your body language and presence naturally become more compelling and influential.

Enhancing body language and presence is a transformative process that empowers you to project confidence, charisma, and authenticity. By focusing on posture and alignment, maintaining eye contact, mastering facial expressions, using purposeful gestures, developing vocal presence, aligning verbal and non-verbal cues, practicing mindfulness, and cultivating confidence and self-belief, you can elevate your body language and presence to make a lasting impact. Remember, your body language and presence are powerful tools that can shape how others perceive you and how you feel about yourself, allowing you to

Building Rapport and Connecting with Others

Building rapport and connecting with others is essential for establishing meaningful relationships, fostering collaboration, and enhancing personal and professional interactions. When you can genuinely connect with others, it not only strengthens your confidence but also creates a positive and supportive environment.

1. Active Listening: Active listening is the foundation of building rapport and connecting with others. It involves giving your full attention to the speaker, demonstrating genuine interest, and showing empathy. Practice active listening by maintaining eye contact, nodding to show understanding, and asking thoughtful questions to encourage further dialogue. By truly listening, you create a safe space for open communication and build trust.

2. Empathy and Understanding: Empathy is the ability to understand and share the feelings of another person. Cultivating empathy allows you to connect on a deeper level with others, demonstrating that you genuinely care about their experiences and perspectives. Put yourself in their shoes, validate their emotions, and respond with kindness and understanding. By showing

empathy, you create a sense of belonging and foster strong connections.

3. Authenticity and Vulnerability: Authenticity is key to building rapport and establishing genuine connections. Be true to yourself and express your thoughts and emotions sincerely. Avoid pretending to be someone you're not or putting up a facade. Embrace vulnerability by sharing your experiences, fears, and challenges. When you show your authentic self, you create an environment that encourages others to do the same, fostering deeper connections.

4. Finding Common Ground: Finding common ground is an effective way to establish rapport and connect with others. Look for shared interests, experiences, or values that you can relate to. Engage in conversations that explore these commonalities, allowing you to bond and create a sense of camaraderie. Finding common ground builds a foundation of mutual understanding and strengthens connections.

5. Non-Judgmental Attitude: Approach interactions with a non-judgmental attitude, accepting others for who they are without imposing preconceived notions or biases. Be open-minded and suspend judgment, allowing space for diverse perspectives and experiences. When you demonstrate non-judgment, you create an inclusive and safe environment where individuals feel valued and respected.

6. Effective Communication: Clear and effective communication is vital for building rapport and connecting with others. Express your thoughts and ideas in a concise and articulate manner, using language that is appropriate for the situation. Be mindful of your tone and body language, ensuring they align with your message. Aim for open and respectful dialogue that encourages active participation and collaboration.

7. Emotional Intelligence: Emotional intelligence is the ability to understand and manage your own emotions and those of others. Develop emotional intelligence by being aware of your own emotions and reactions, as well as being sensitive to the emotions of others. Adapt your communication style and approach based on the emotional cues of the individuals you are interacting with. Emotional intelligence enhances your ability to connect on an emotional level.

8. Follow-up and Nurturing Relationships: Building rapport and connecting with others is an on-going process that requires nurturing relationships over time. Follow up with individuals you have connected with, whether through a simple check-in or by continuing the conversation. Show genuine interest in their well-being and celebrate their successes. By investing time and effort in maintaining relationships, you deepen connections and build a strong network of support.

Building rapport and connecting with others is a skill that can enrich your personal and professional life. By practicing active listening, cultivating empathy, embracing authenticity and vulnerability, finding common ground, adopting a non-judgmental attitude, honing effective communication, developing emotional intelligence, and nurturing relationships, you can create meaningful connections that foster trust, collaboration, and personal growth.

8

Cultivating Belief in Yourself: The Power of a Growth Mind-Set

Believing in your-self is crucial for personal growth, resilience, and achieving success. A growth Mind-set is the foundation for cultivating this belief, as it embraces the idea that abilities and intelligence can be developed through dedication and effort.

Believing in yourself is a fundamental aspect of building confidence and achieving personal success. Here are some strategies to enhance your belief in yourself:

1. Recognize your strengths: Take inventory of your skills, talents, and achievements. Recognize what you excel at and what sets you apart. Celebrate your successes and acknowledge your capabilities. Remind yourself of these strengths regularly.
2. Challenge self-doubt: Identify and challenge self-doubt and negative self-talk. Notice when negative thoughts or limiting beliefs arise and consciously replace them with positive affirmations and constructive self-talk. Reframe your self-perception to focus on your potential and possibilities.
3. Set realistic goals: Set achievable goals that align with your values and aspirations. Break down larger goals into smaller, manageable steps. Accomplishing these goals will reinforce your belief in your abilities and build momentum.

4. Celebrate progress: Celebrate even the smallest victories along your journey. Acknowledge your progress and achievements, no matter how insignificant they may seem. Recognizing and celebrating milestones will reinforce your belief in your ability to succeed.
5. Surround yourself with support: Surround yourself with people who believe in you and support your aspirations. Seek out mentors, friends, or family members who provide encouragement, constructive feedback, and positive energy. Their belief in you can help bolster your own self-belief.
6. Embrace failure as a learning opportunity: Understand that failure is a natural part of growth and success. View setbacks as learning experiences rather than reflections of your worth or abilities. Embrace the lessons learned from failures and use them as stepping stones for improvement.
7. Practice self-compassion: Be kind to yourself and practice self-compassion. Treat yourself with the same understanding, patience, and support you would offer to a friend. Recognize that everyone makes mistakes and faces challenges, and that it is okay to be imperfect.
8. Visualize success: Engage in visualization exercises where you vividly imagine yourself achieving your goals and living a fulfilling life. Visualize the confident, capable, and successful version of yourself. This practice can help reinforce positive beliefs and build confidence.
9. Take calculated risks: Step outside your comfort zone and take calculated risks. Push yourself to try new things and embrace challenges. Each time you step outside your comfort zone and succeed, your belief in your abilities will grow.
10. Practice self-care: Take care of your physical, mental, and emotional well-being. Engage in activities that

nourish and energize you. Prioritize self-care to maintain a positive Mind-set, which will strengthen your belief in yourself.

11. Understanding the Growth Mind-set: A growth Mind-set is the belief that talents, abilities, and intelligence can be developed through hard work, practice, and learning from setbacks. It contrasts with a fixed Mind-set, which assumes that abilities are fixed and cannot be changed. Embracing a growth Mind-set opens up possibilities, encourages continuous improvement, and fuels belief in your potential.

12. Embracing Challenges and Seeing Failure as Learning Opportunities: Challenges and failures are opportunities for growth and learning. Embrace challenges as a chance to stretch your abilities and develop new skills. When faced with setbacks, view them as valuable lessons rather than personal shortcomings. Shift your perspective from "I can't do it" to "I haven't mastered it yet." By reframing challenges and failures, you build resilience and strengthen your belief in yourself.

13. Practicing Self-Compassion and Positive Self-Talk: Self-compassion and positive self-talk are essential for cultivating belief in yourself. Treat yourself with kindness and understanding when faced with difficulties or setbacks. Replace self-criticism with self-encouragement and affirmations. Challenge negative thoughts and replace them with positive and empowering statements. By nurturing self-compassion and positive self-talk, you build a foundation of belief and self-confidence.

14. Celebrating Progress and Small Wins: Acknowledge and celebrate your progress and small wins along the way. Recognize that personal growth is a journey, and every step forward is an achievement. Take time to

appreciate your efforts, no matter how small they may seem. By celebrating progress, you reinforce belief in your ability to learn and grow.

15. Seeking Growth-Oriented Feedback: Seek feedback from others who can provide constructive and growth-oriented perspectives. Be open to receiving feedback and view it as an opportunity for growth rather than criticism. Incorporate feedback into your self-improvement journey, adjusting your approach and strategies accordingly. By actively seeking feedback, you demonstrate a commitment to continuous learning and development.
16. Surrounding Yourself with Supportive Individuals: Surround yourself with supportive individuals who believe in your potential and encourage your growth. Seek out mentors, friends, or colleagues who inspire and motivate you. Engage in communities or groups that foster a growth Mind-set and provide a positive environment for personal development. By surrounding yourself with supportive individuals, you create a network that reinforces belief in yourself.
17. Setting Realistic and Stretching Goals: Set realistic goals that challenge you to step out of your comfort zone while still being attainable. Break down larger goals into smaller, actionable steps. By setting and achieving these goals, you build evidence of your capabilities and strengthen belief in yourself. Stretch yourself beyond what you think you are capable of, as this expands your understanding of your potential.
18. Persistence and Resilience: Belief in yourself requires persistence and resilience. Understand that progress and success often involve setbacks and obstacles. Maintain a Mind-set of perseverance, embracing challenges and setbacks as opportunities for growth. Cultivate resilience by bouncing back from failures and

maintaining a positive attitude. By persisting through challenges, you reinforce your belief in yourself and your ability to overcome obstacles.

Remember that building self-belief is a journey that requires patience and consistent effort. By implementing these strategies and consciously choosing to believe in yourself, you can cultivate a strong sense of self-confidence and unlock your full potential. Cultivating belief in yourself through a growth mind-set is a transformative process that empowers you to achieve personal and professional success.

The Power of Growth Mind-set

The power of a growth mind-set lies in the belief that our abilities and intelligence can be developed through dedication, effort, and continuous learning. It is the understanding that our qualities are not fixed traits but can be cultivated and improved over time. Here are some key aspects of the power of a growth mind-set:

1. Embracing challenges: People with a growth Mind-set see challenges as opportunities for growth and learning. They view setbacks as temporary and approach them with resilience and determination. Instead of avoiding challenges, they actively seek them out to expand their abilities.
2. Persistence and effort: Those with a growth Mind-set understand that effort and persistence are key to achieving success. They believe that hard work, practice, and perseverance can lead to improvement and mastery. They are willing to put in the time and effort required to reach their goals.
3. Embracing failure as a learning opportunity: Rather than being discouraged by failure, individuals with a growth mind-set see it as an opportunity for learning and development. They understand that failure is a

natural part of the learning process and use it as a stepping stone for improvement. They analyze their mistakes, make adjustments, and strive to do better next time.

4. Emphasizing the process over outcomes: Rather than solely focusing on the end result, individuals with a growth mind-set value the learning process itself. They understand that progress is more important than immediate success and that true growth comes from the journey. They set goals, create strategies, and enjoy the process of learning and improving.
5. Seeking feedback and embracing criticism: People with a growth mind-set actively seek feedback from others, valuing it as an opportunity to learn and grow. They are open to constructive criticism and use it to identify areas for improvement. They see feedback as valuable input for their personal and professional development.
6. Cultivating a love for learning: Individuals with a growth mind-set have a deep appreciation for learning. They see knowledge and skills as valuable assets that can be continually expanded. They have a curiosity and desire to acquire new knowledge, develop new skills, and explore new areas of interest.
7. Overcoming obstacles and setbacks: A growth Mind-set allows individuals to overcome obstacles and setbacks with resilience and determination. They view challenges as temporary roadblocks that can be overcome with effort and strategic problem-solving. They persist in the face of adversity and use setbacks as opportunities for growth.
8. Embracing collaboration and learning from others: People with a growth Mind-set value collaboration and recognize the importance of learning from others. They seek out diverse perspectives and actively engage in collaborative efforts. They understand that working

with others can enhance their own learning and contribute to collective growth.

9. Cultivating self-belief: A growth mind-set fosters a strong sense of self-belief and confidence. By understanding that abilities can be developed, individuals with a growth Mind-set approach new tasks and challenges with a positive attitude. They believe in their own potential and have the confidence to take on new opportunities.
10. Continual improvement: A growth mind-set is characterized by a commitment to continuous improvement. Individuals with a growth mind-set are never satisfied with the status quo and consistently strive to enhance their skills, knowledge, and abilities. They embrace lifelong learning and are open to new experiences and challenges.

By adopting a growth mind-set, individuals unlock their potential, embrace challenges, and continuously learn and improve. It allows for greater resilience, personal growth, and the realization of one's full capabilities.

Embracing a Growth Mind-set for Personal and Professional Growth

Embracing a growth Mind-set is a powerful Mind-set shift that can unlock your potential for personal and professional growth. It is the belief that talents, abilities, and intelligence can be developed through dedication, effort, and a willingness to learn. Embracing a growth Mind-set is essential for personal growth and development. Here are some ways to cultivate and embrace a growth Mind-set for your own growth:

1. Embrace challenges: Instead of avoiding challenges, actively seek out opportunities that push you outside your comfort zone. Embrace challenges as a chance to learn, grow, and develop new skills.

2. View failures as learning experiences: Shift your perspective on failure. Instead of seeing it as a setback or a reflection of your abilities, view it as a valuable learning experience. Analyze what went wrong, identify lessons learned, and use that knowledge to improve and adapt.
3. Cultivate a love for learning: Foster a curiosity and thirst for knowledge. Seek out opportunities to learn new things, whether through reading, taking courses, attending workshops, or engaging in new experiences. Embrace the Mind-set that learning is a lifelong journey.
4. Develop resilience: Build your resilience by understanding that setbacks and obstacles are part of the growth process. Rather than becoming discouraged, find ways to bounce back, adapt, and persevere. See challenges as opportunities to develop your resilience and inner strength.
5. Embrace effort and perseverance: Understand that effort and persistence are essential for growth. Embrace the Mind-set that hard work, practice, and dedication are what lead to improvement and success. Celebrate your progress and the effort you put into your endeavors.
6. Seek feedback and constructive criticism: Actively seek feedback from others and be open to constructive criticism. Feedback provides valuable insights and perspectives that can help you identify areas for improvement and refine your skills. Use feedback as a tool for growth and development.
7. Surround yourself with growth-minded individuals: Surround yourself with people who embody a growth Mind-set. Engage in discussions and collaborations with individuals who encourage growth, inspire you, and challenge your thinking. Their Mind-set and energy can positively influence your own growth journey.

8. Set meaningful goals: Set goals that align with your passions, values, and aspirations. Break them down into smaller, achievable steps and track your progress along the way. Setbacks may occur, but use them as opportunities to recalibrate and adjust your approach.
9. Practice self-reflection: Regularly take time for self-reflection and introspection. Assess your strengths, weaknesses, and areas for growth. Celebrate your achievements and acknowledge areas where you can further develop. Use this self-awareness to guide your growth journey.
10. Maintain a positive Mind-set: Cultivate a positive Mind-set by focusing on possibilities and opportunities rather than limitations. Challenge negative self-talk and replace it with affirmations and positive thoughts. Embrace optimism and believe in your ability to learn, grow, and overcome challenges.
11. The Benefits of a Growth Mind-set: A growth Mind-set opens doors to personal and professional growth by fostering resilience, adaptability, and a love for learning. It allows you to embrace challenges, view failures as opportunities for growth, and persist in the face of setbacks. With a growth Mind-set, you are more likely to take risks, develop new skills, and achieve higher levels of success and fulfillment.
12. Recognizing and Challenging Fixed Mind-set Traps: Fixed Mind-set traps are limiting beliefs that hinder personal and professional growth. Recognize these traps, such as the fear of failure, the need for validation, or the belief in innate talent, and challenge them. Replace fixed Mind-set thoughts with growth-oriented perspectives, focusing on effort, learning, and continuous improvement.
13. Embracing Challenges and Learning Opportunities: Embrace challenges as opportunities for growth and

learning. Instead of avoiding difficult tasks, approach them with a growth Mind-set. See them as chances to develop new skills and expand your capabilities. Embrace a love for learning, seeking out new knowledge and experiences. Emphasize the process of learning and growth rather than solely focusing on outcomes.

14. Reframing Failure as Feedback and Learning: Reframe failure as feedback and an opportunity for learning. Rather than viewing failures as indications of personal shortcomings, see them as valuable lessons that provide insights into areas for improvement. Analyze what went wrong, extract the lessons learned, and use them to adjust your approach. Embrace the idea that failure is a natural part of the learning and growth process.
15. Cultivating a Positive and Resilient Mind-set: Cultivate a positive and resilient Mind-set by developing self-awareness and self-compassion. Be mindful of your thoughts and self-talk, replacing negative and self-limiting beliefs with positive and empowering ones. Practice self-compassion by being kind to yourself in the face of challenges and setbacks. Nurture a Mind-set that promotes growth, resilience, and self-belief.
16. Embracing Continuous Learning and Skill Development: Adopt a Mind-set of continuous learning and skill development. Seek out opportunities to acquire new knowledge, develop new skills, and expand your expertise. Embrace a growth-oriented approach to personal and professional development, setting goals that challenge you and push you beyond your comfort zone. Actively seek feedback and seek ways to improve and refine your abilities.
17. Seeking Feedback and Embracing Growth-Oriented Criticism: Seek feedback from others and embrace growth-oriented criticism. Actively seek out individuals who can provide constructive feedback and different

perspectives. Be open to receiving feedback, even if it may be uncomfortable at times. Use feedback as a catalyst for growth, making adjustments and improvements based on the insights gained.

18. Cultivating a Supportive Network and Collaboration: Surround yourself with a supportive network of individuals who share and encourage a growth Mind-set. Collaborate with others who have diverse skills and expertise, fostering an environment of shared learning and growth. Engage in meaningful conversations, exchange ideas, and seek opportunities for collaboration. The collective wisdom and support of a network can fuel personal and professional growth.

Remember, embracing a growth Mind-set is an ongoing process that requires consistent effort and self-reflection. By adopting this Mind-set, you open yourself up to endless possibilities for growth, development, and personal fulfillment. Embracing a growth Mind-set is a transformative journey that empowers you to achieve continuous personal and professional growth. By recognizing fixed Mind-set traps, embracing challenges, reframing failure,

Overcoming Imposter Syndrome and Self-doubt

Imposter syndrome and self-doubt are common challenges that many people face, regardless of their accomplishments or abilities. Imposter syndrome refers to the feeling of being a fraud or not deserving of one's successes, despite evidence to the contrary. Self-doubt, on the other hand, involves questioning one's abilities, worth, or competence. Overcoming imposter syndrome and self-doubt requires self-awareness, self-compassion, and proactive strategies. In this journey, individuals can learn to recognize and challenge their negative self-perceptions, build self-confidence, and embrace their true capabilities. By addressing these challenges, individuals can unlock their full potential and pursue their goals with greater confidence and authenticity. Imposter syndrome and self-doubt can be significant barriers to personal and professional growth. They can hinder your confidence, hinder your ability to take risks, and undermine your achievements.

1. Recognizing Imposter Syndrome: Imposter syndrome is a feeling of inadequacy and self-doubt despite evidence of your skills and accomplishments. Recognize the signs of imposter syndrome, such as discounting your achievements, attributing success to luck, and fearing being exposed as a fraud. Acknowledging imposter syndrome is the first step in overcoming it.

2. Challenge Negative Self-Talk: Negative self-talk fuels self-doubt and perpetuates imposter syndrome. Become aware of your inner critic and challenge negative thoughts. Replace self-critical thoughts with positive and empowering statements. Focus on your strengths, accomplishments, and the value you bring. Practice self-compassion and kindness toward yourself.

3. Reframe Failure and Setbacks: Reframe failure and setbacks as opportunities for growth and learning. Instead of seeing them as proof of your inadequacy, view them as stepping stones on your journey to success. Embrace a growth Mind-set and see failures as valuable lessons that can contribute to your personal and professional development.

4. Celebrate Your Achievements: Acknowledge and celebrate your achievements, no matter how small they may seem. Keep a record of your successes, compliments, and positive feedback. Remind yourself of the skills, knowledge, and experience that you possess. Reflecting on your accomplishments can boost your self-confidence and provide a counterbalance to self-doubt.

5. Seek Support and Share Your Feelings: Reach out for support from trusted friends, mentors, or colleagues.

Share your feelings of self-doubt and imposter syndrome with individuals who can provide encouragement and perspective. Often, you will find that others have experienced similar doubts, and their insights and support can help you overcome them.

6. Practice Self-Reflection and Self-Awareness: Engage in self-reflection to gain a deeper understanding of your strengths, values, and goals. Recognize and challenge any unrealistic expectations you may have set for yourself. Cultivate self-awareness to identify patterns of self-doubt and imposter syndrome. By understanding yourself better, you can address and overcome these challenges more effectively.
7. Embrace Continuous Learning: Commit to lifelong learning and skill development. Invest in your personal and professional growth by seeking out new knowledge, training, and experiences. As you expand your expertise and competence, you will gain confidence in your abilities. Emphasize the process of learning rather than solely focusing on outcomes.
8. Take Action and Embrace Discomfort: Challenge yourself to step out of your comfort zone and take action despite feelings of self-doubt. Recognize that discomfort and fear are natural when pursuing growth and new opportunities. Take small steps and gradually increase your comfort zone. As you push through self-doubt and take action, you will build resilience and self-confidence.

Overcoming imposter syndrome and self-doubt is a journey of self-discovery and growth. By recognizing imposter syndrome, challenging negative self-talk, reframing failure, celebrating achievements, seeking support, practicing self-reflection, embracing continuous learning, and taking action, you can overcome these barriers and cultivate self-confidence. Remember, you are capable and deserving of success, and your true potential lies beyond the grip of self-doubt.

Building Resilience and Perseverance in the Face of Challenges

Life is full of challenges and obstacles that can test our resolve and shake our confidence. Building resilience and perseverance is essential for navigating these difficulties with strength and determination. It is crucial for navigating challenges and setbacks effectively. Here are some strategies to help you develop resilience and perseverance:

1. Reframe challenges as opportunities: Instead of viewing challenges as insurmountable obstacles, reframe them as opportunities for growth and learning. Embrace a mind-set that sees challenges as a chance to develop new skills, gain experience, and become stronger.
2. Cultivate a positive mind-set: Foster a positive and optimistic outlook on life. Focus on the possibilities and potential for growth rather than dwelling on negative aspects. Train your mind to see setbacks as temporary and believe in your ability to overcome them.
3. Set realistic expectations: Establish realistic expectations for yourself and the challenges you face. Understand that progress may take time and setbacks are a normal part of the journey. Set achievable goals and celebrate small victories along the way.
4. Build a strong support system: Surround yourself with supportive and positive individuals who can offer encouragement, guidance, and perspective during challenging times. Seek out mentors, friends, or family members who believe in you and can provide emotional support.
5. Practice self-care: Take care of your physical, mental, and emotional well-being. Engage in activities that recharge and rejuvenate you, such as exercise, meditation, hobbies, or spending time in nature.

Prioritize self-care to build resilience and maintain a positive mind-set.

6. Develop problem-solving skills: Enhance your problem-solving skills to approach challenges with a proactive mind-set. Break down problems into smaller, manageable steps and explore different strategies and solutions. Seek out advice or perspectives from others to expand your problem-solving repertoire.
7. Embrace failure as a learning opportunity: Recognize that failure is a natural part of the learning and growth process. Instead of being discouraged by failures, view them as opportunities for reflection and learning. Extract lessons from setbacks and use them to refine your approach.
8. Practice self-reflection: Regularly reflect on your experiences and challenges. Analyze your responses, strengths, and areas for improvement. Use this self-reflection to identify patterns, learn from past experiences, and develop strategies for resilience and perseverance.
9. Cultivate adaptability: Be open to change and adaptable in the face of challenges. Embrace flexibility and willingness to adjust your plans or strategies when needed. Adaptability allows you to navigate unexpected obstacles and find alternative pathways to success.
10. Celebrate progress and small victories: Acknowledge and celebrate your progress, no matter how small. Recognize the effort and resilience you have demonstrated. Celebrating milestones and accomplishments boosts your confidence and motivation to persevere.
11. Understanding Resilience: Resilience is the ability to bounce back from setbacks, adapt to change, and maintain a positive outlook. It involves developing emotional strength, coping mechanisms, and the ability

to learn and grow from challenges. Recognize that resilience is a skill that can be cultivated and honed.

12. Cultivating a Growth Mind-set: Adopting a growth Mind-set is foundational to building resilience. Embrace challenges as opportunities for growth and learning. See setbacks as temporary and solvable obstacles. Believe in your ability to improve and overcome difficulties through effort, persistence, and learning from failures.

13. Building a Supportive Network: Surround yourself with a supportive network of friends, family, mentors, and colleagues who can provide encouragement, advice, and assistance during challenging times. Share your struggles with trusted individuals who can offer different perspectives and help you navigate obstacles. Lean on their support when needed.

14. Practicing Self-Care: Prioritize self-care to strengthen your resilience. Take care of your physical, emotional, and mental well-being. Engage in activities that recharge and rejuvenate you. Prioritize sleep, exercise, healthy eating, and relaxation techniques. Nurturing your well-being provides a solid foundation for facing challenges with resilience.

15. Developing Emotional Intelligence: Cultivate emotional intelligence to better understand and manage your emotions during challenging situations. Develop self-awareness to recognize your emotional triggers and responses. Practice emotional regulation techniques, such as deep breathing, mindfulness, and reframing negative thoughts. Enhancing emotional intelligence helps you navigate challenges with a calm and balanced Mind-set.

16. Seeking Meaning and Perspective: Seek meaning and purpose in the face of challenges. Reflect on the lessons and growth opportunities that difficult situations can

offer. Consider how the experience can contribute to your personal development and align with your values. Adopting a broader perspective helps to maintain a positive outlook and resilience in the face of adversity.

17. Setting Realistic Goals and Taking Incremental Steps: Set realistic goals and break them down into manageable steps. Rather than becoming overwhelmed by the enormity of a challenge, focus on the next actionable step. Celebrate small victories along the way, as they reinforce your resilience and perseverance. Gradually build momentum and progress toward your goals.
18. Embracing Failure as a Stepping Stone to Success: Shift your perception of failure from a negative outcome to a valuable learning experience. Embrace failure as an opportunity for growth, adaptation, and refinement of your approach. Learn from your mistakes, make adjustments, and persevere. Each failure brings you closer to success.
19. Cultivating Optimism and Gratitude: Cultivate optimism and gratitude as a way to maintain a positive Mind-set in the face of challenges. Focus on what you can control and find reasons to be grateful, even in difficult times. Adopting an optimistic perspective helps you stay motivated, resilient, and focused on finding solutions.
20. Learning from Role Models and Inspiring Stories: Seek inspiration from role models and stories of individuals who have overcome adversity. Read biographies, listen to podcasts, or engage in conversations with those who have faced and triumphed over challenges. Their stories serve as a reminder of the human capacity for resilience and perseverance.

Building resilience and perseverance is a lifelong journey that equips you with the strength and determination to navigate challenges. Remember that building resilience and perseverance is a continuous process. Each challenge you face provides an opportunity to strengthen these qualities. With time, practice, and a positive mind-set, you can develop the resilience and perseverance needed to overcome obstacles and achieve your goals.

9

Surrounding Yourself with Positivity: Nurturing Supportive Relationships

Surrounding yourself with positivity is a powerful practice that can greatly enhance your well-being and outlook on life. It involves intentionally creating an environment that promotes positivity, uplifting energy, and a constructive mind-set. By surrounding yourself with positive influences, thoughts, and experiences, you can cultivate a more optimistic and resilient approach to life's challenges.

The people you choose to spend time with play a significant role in your well-being. Surrounding yourself with positive, supportive individuals who uplift and inspire you can have a profound impact on your mind-set and overall happiness. These individuals can provide encouragement, offer different perspectives, and serve as a source of motivation during both the ups and downs of life.

Creating a positive physical environment is equally important. Your surroundings can influence your mood and mind-set. Consider organizing and decorating your physical space in a way that brings you joy and tranquility. Use colors, scents, and lighting that uplift your spirits. Surround yourself with items that hold positive associations or represent your goals and aspirations.

Engaging in activities that bring you joy and fulfillment is another way to surround yourself with positivity. Pursue hobbies, interests, and passions that energize and inspire you. These activities provide an outlet for self-expression and personal growth, allowing you to tap into your strengths and cultivate a positive mind-set.

Practicing gratitude is a powerful tool for cultivating positivity. Taking time each day to reflect on the things you are grateful for helps shift your focus toward the positive aspects of your life. It trains your mind to appreciate the present moment and fosters a sense of contentment and appreciation for the blessings in your life.

Limiting your exposure to negative influences, such as negative media or toxic relationships, is crucial. Be mindful of the media you consume and the conversations you engage in. Choose to surround yourself with content and conversations that inspire, educate, and uplift you. This helps protect your mind-set and create a space for positivity to flourish.

By consciously surrounding yourself with positivity, you can develop a more optimistic and resilient mind-set. This practice allows you to approach challenges with a constructive perspective, seek opportunities for growth and learning, and maintain a sense of gratitude and joy in your daily life. Remember, it's an ongoing process that requires self-awareness and intentional choices, but the rewards are well worth the effort.

Nurturing supportive relationships is essential for our overall well-being and personal growth. These relationships provide a sense of belonging, understanding, and encouragement, and they play a vital role in our emotional, mental, and even physical health. When we surround ourselves with supportive individuals, we create a network of people who uplift us, celebrate our successes, and provide comfort during challenging times.

Supportive relationships are built on trust, empathy, and mutual respect. They involve open and honest communication, active listening, and a willingness to support one another's needs and goals. These relationships provide a safe space for vulnerability and sharing our true selves without fear of judgment or rejection.

Supportive relationships come in various forms. They can include close friends, family members, romantic partners, mentors, or colleagues who share common interests and values. These relationships thrive when there is a genuine connection, shared experiences, and a commitment to each other's well-being.

Nurturing supportive relationships involves both giving and receiving support. It requires being present for others, offering a listening ear, and providing empathy and encouragement. It also means being willing to ask for help and allowing others to support us when needed. In these relationships, both parties contribute to each other's growth and provide a sense of validation and affirmation.

Supportive relationships have numerous benefits. They provide emotional support, helping us navigate life's challenges and setbacks. They offer a sense of belonging and reduce feelings of loneliness and isolation. Supportive relationships also foster personal growth and self-confidence by providing constructive feedback, motivation, and guidance.

To nurture supportive relationships, it's important to invest time and effort in building and maintaining them. This involves being reliable, showing appreciation, and being responsive to others' needs. It also means respecting boundaries, communicating openly, and resolving conflicts in a healthy and respectful manner.

Ultimately, nurturing supportive relationships enriches our lives and contributes to our overall well-being. These relationships provide a strong support system, enhance our sense of self-worth, and create lasting connections that bring joy and fulfillment. By prioritizing the cultivation of supportive relationships, we can experience greater happiness, resilience, and a sense of belonging in our journey through life.

The people we surround ourselves with have a significant impact on our well-being, Mind-set, and overall outlook on life. Nurturing supportive relationships and surrounding ourselves with positivity can foster personal growth, boost confidence, and enhance our overall quality of life.

Surrounding yourself with positivity is essential for maintaining a healthy mind-set and promoting personal well-being. Here are some strategies to help you cultivate a positive environment:

1. Choose your social circle wisely: Surround yourself with positive, supportive, and uplifting individuals who inspire and motivate you. Seek out friends, family members, or mentors who radiate positivity and share your values. Distance yourself from toxic or negative influences that bring you down.
2. Engage in positive activities: Participate in activities that bring you joy, fulfillment, and positive energy. Engage in hobbies, sports, or creative pursuits that uplift your spirits and create a positive atmosphere. Surround yourself with things that inspire and ignite your passions.
3. Practice gratitude: Cultivate a habit of gratitude by regularly acknowledging and appreciating the positive aspects of your life. Take time each day to reflect on the things you are grateful for, whether big or small. This practice helps shift your focus toward the positive aspects of life and fosters a positive mind-set.
4. Limit exposure to negative media: Be mindful of the media you consume, including news, social media, and entertainment. Limit your exposure to negative content that can contribute to a pessimistic outlook. Choose to engage with media that uplifts, educates, and inspires you.

5. Create a positive physical environment: Organize and decorate your physical space in a way that promotes positivity and relaxation. Surround yourself with items that have positive associations or bring you joy. Use colors, scents, and lighting that uplift your mood and create a welcoming atmosphere.
6. Practice positive self-talk: Pay attention to your internal dialogue and replace negative self-talk with positive affirmations and self-encouragement. Challenge self-limiting beliefs and replace them with empowering statements. Be kind and compassionate to yourself in your thoughts and words.
7. Seek out inspirational resources: Read books, listen to podcasts, or watch videos that inspire and uplift you. Choose resources that promote personal growth, positivity, and resilience. Surround yourself with inspiring stories and messages that encourage you to reach your full potential.
8. Engage in acts of kindness: Participate in acts of kindness and generosity toward others. Helping others not only brings joy to their lives but also fosters a sense of positivity within yourself. Volunteer, offer support to friends or family, or engage in random acts of kindness in your community.
9. Practice self-care: Prioritize self-care activities that nourish your physical, mental, and emotional well-being. Engage in activities that promote relaxation, stress reduction, and self-reflection. Take time for activities that bring you joy, such as practicing mindfulness, exercising, or pursuing hobbies.
10. Monitor your thoughts and emotions: Be mindful of your thoughts and emotions throughout the day. Notice when negativity arises and consciously choose to shift your focus toward positive thoughts. Practice

techniques such as deep breathing, meditation, or journaling to cultivate positivity and manage stress.

11. The Power of Supportive Relationships: Supportive relationships provide a sense of belonging, encouragement, and emotional support. They offer a safe space to share our thoughts, fears, and aspirations. Surrounding ourselves with positive and uplifting individuals can boost our self-esteem, inspire us to reach our goals, and provide valuable guidance during challenging times.
12. Assessing Your Relationships: Evaluate your current relationships and assess their impact on your well-being. Identify individuals who uplift and inspire you, and those who may drain your energy or promote negativity. Consider the values and qualities you seek in your relationships, and determine if your current connections align with those ideals.
13. Cultivating Positivity in Existing Relationships: Foster positivity in your existing relationships by practicing empathy, active listening, and expressing gratitude. Show genuine interest in others' lives and experiences, and offer support and encouragement when needed. Celebrate their achievements and strengths, creating a positive and uplifting dynamic within the relationship.
14. Setting Boundaries and Surrounding Yourself with Positive Influences: Establishing healthy boundaries is essential for maintaining positive relationships. Learn to say no when necessary and prioritize your well-being. Surround yourself with individuals who share your values, inspire you, and uplift your spirits. Seek out positive influences in various areas of your life, such as work, hobbies, and personal interests.
15. Building a Supportive Network: Actively seek to build a supportive network by reaching out to like-minded

individuals, joining communities or groups aligned with your interests, and attending events or gatherings where you can connect with people who share your values. Engage in meaningful conversations, share your aspirations, and be open to supporting others in their journey as well.

16. Being a Positive Influence: Nurture positivity within your relationships by being a positive influence yourself. Be mindful of your words and actions, choosing kindness, empathy, and encouragement. Celebrate the successes and strengths of others, offering support and assistance when needed. By radiating positivity, you can inspire and uplift those around you.
17. Letting Go of Toxic Relationships: Recognize when a relationship becomes toxic or consistently negative, and be willing to let go. It can be challenging, but prioritizing your well-being is crucial. Surrounding yourself with positivity means distancing yourself from individuals who consistently bring you down or hinder your growth. Focus on nurturing relationships that uplift and support your journey.
18. Seeking Professional Support: In some cases, professional support may be necessary to navigate challenging relationships or heal from past wounds. Consider seeking guidance from therapists, counselors, or coaches who can provide valuable insights, tools, and techniques to help you foster healthier and more positive connections.

Nurturing supportive relationships and surrounding yourself with positivity is a powerful catalyst for personal growth, happiness, and resilience. By assessing your relationships, cultivating positivity, setting boundaries, building a supportive network, and being a positive influence, you can create a supportive environment that uplifts and empowers you. Remember, the relationships you cultivate have the power to shape your life, so choose wisely and invest in connections that nurture your well-being and contribute to your growth.

Remember, surrounding yourself with positivity is an ongoing practice that requires conscious effort and self-awareness. By intentionally creating a positive environment, you can enhance your overall well-being, increase your resilience, and better navigate life's challenges.

Identifying Toxic Relationships and their Impact on Selfesteem

Identifying toxic relationships is an important step towards protecting our well-being and fostering healthy connections with others. Toxic relationships are characterized by unhealthy dynamics that cause harm, negativity, and emotional distress. These relationships can have a detrimental impact on our mental and emotional health, self-esteem, and overall quality of life.

Toxic relationships can manifest in various forms, including friendships, romantic partnerships, family relationships, or even professional connections. They are often marked by behaviors such as constant criticism, manipulation, disrespect, control, dishonesty, and lack of empathy. These negative patterns can erode trust, create a sense of fear or insecurity, and drain our emotional energy.

Recognizing toxic relationships involves paying attention to warning signs and evaluating how these relationships make us feel. Some common indicators include feeling constantly drained, anxious, or depressed when interacting with the person, experiencing a lack of support or emotional validation, and encountering frequent conflicts or power imbalances.

Identifying toxic relationships also requires examining how the relationship impacts our well-being and personal growth. If a relationship consistently brings us down, hinders our progress, or compromises our values and boundaries, it may be a sign of toxicity.

Once we identify a toxic relationship, it is crucial to take steps to protect ourselves and prioritize our well-being. This may involve setting boundaries, asserting ourselves, or even distancing ourselves from the person if necessary. Seeking support from trusted friends, family, or professionals can also provide guidance and perspective during this process.

By recognizing toxic relationships, we can create space for healthier connections in our lives. Surrounding ourselves with positive, supportive, and nurturing relationships contributes to our happiness, personal growth, and overall well-being. It allows us to cultivate connections that uplift us, promote mutual respect, and encourage our authentic selves to thrive.

When we are involved in toxic relationships, where there is consistent criticism, manipulation, and disrespect, our self-esteem can suffer greatly.

Toxic relationships often involve emotional abuse, where the other person intentionally undermines our confidence and self-worth. They may belittle our accomplishments, invalidate our feelings, or constantly criticize and find fault with us. Over time, this constant negativity can erode our self-esteem and make us doubt our own abilities, worthiness, and value as a person.

Being in a toxic relationship can also lead to feelings of powerlessness and dependency. The toxic person may exert control over us, making us feel incapable of making decisions or taking action on our own. This can diminish our self-esteem, as we begin to doubt our ability to navigate life independently and effectively.

Furthermore, toxic relationships can create a cycle of self-blame and self-doubt. The toxic person may shift blame onto us, making us feel responsible for their negative behavior or the problems in the relationship. We may internalize this blame, believing that we are inherently flawed or deserving of mistreatment, further damaging our self-esteem.

The impact of toxic relationships on self-esteem can extend beyond the specific relationship itself. The negative beliefs and self-perception developed within the toxic dynamic can spill over into other areas of our lives. We may begin to doubt our abilities in various aspects, feel unworthy of healthy relationships, or struggle with assertiveness and setting boundaries.

It is crucial to recognize the detrimental impact of toxic relationships on our self-esteem and take steps to protect ourselves. This may involve seeking support from trusted friends, family, or professionals who can provide validation and perspective. It also means setting boundaries and distancing ourselves from toxic individuals to create space for healing and rebuilding our self-esteem.

By freeing ourselves from toxic relationships and nurturing healthy connections, we can begin to rebuild our self-esteem. Surrounding ourselves with supportive and positive influences, practicing self-compassion, and engaging in activities that promote self-growth and self-care can all contribute to rebuilding our self-esteem and regaining our sense of self-worth.

Toxic relationships can have a detrimental impact on our self-esteem, emotional well-being, and overall quality of life. It is essential to identify and address toxic relationships to protect our self-esteem and foster healthy connections.

1. Recognizing Signs of Toxic Relationships: To identify toxic relationships, be aware of the following signs:

    - Constant criticism and belittling: If someone consistently puts you down, undermines your accomplishments, or criticizes your choices, it may be a sign of a toxic relationship.

- Lack of respect and boundaries: When your boundaries are consistently disregarded, and your feelings and needs are not respected, it can indicate a toxic dynamic.
- Manipulation and control: Manipulative behavior, such as guilt-tripping, gaslighting, or controlling actions, can be indicators of a toxic relationship.
- One-sided and unbalanced relationships: If the relationship feels overwhelmingly one-sided, with little reciprocity or support, it may be unhealthy.
- Constant negativity and drama: If the relationship is characterized by constant negativity, conflict, and drama, it can drain your energy and impact your self-esteem.

2. Understanding the Impact on Self-Esteem: Toxic relationships can significantly impact your self-esteem. Constant criticism, belittlement, and disregard for your boundaries can erode your self-worth over time. The negative energy, manipulation, and control in toxic relationships can make you doubt yourself, feel inadequate, and diminish your confidence. It is important to recognize how toxic relationships affect your self-esteem to take necessary steps towards healing.
3. Setting Boundaries and Prioritizing Self-Care: Establishing clear boundaries is crucial in dealing with toxic relationships. Communicate your needs, assertively express your boundaries, and be firm in enforcing them. Prioritize self-care by engaging in activities that nurture your well-being and self-esteem. Surround yourself with positive influences and seek support from trusted friends, family, or professionals.
4. Seeking Communication and Resolution: In some cases, addressing the toxic behavior through open and honest

communication may be possible. Express your concerns, feelings, and boundaries calmly and assertively. However, be prepared for the possibility that the toxic individual may not be receptive or willing to change. Your well-being should remain the priority.

5. Detaching and Letting Go: If the toxic relationship persists despite attempts to address it, it may be necessary to detach and let go. Understand that you cannot change others, and it is not your responsibility to endure toxic behavior. Detaching may involve limiting contact, creating emotional distance, or even ending the relationship if it is necessary for your well-being.
6. Seeking Professional Support: Dealing with toxic relationships can be challenging, and seeking professional support can be immensely helpful. A therapist or counselor can provide guidance, perspective, and tools to navigate the emotional complexities of toxic relationships and rebuild self-esteem.
7. Surrounding Yourself with Supportive Relationships: As you address toxic relationships, actively seek out and nurture supportive and healthy relationships. Surround yourself with individuals who uplift and support you, respect your boundaries, and contribute positively to your self-esteem. Cultivate connections that encourage personal growth and foster a sense of well-being.

Identifying and addressing toxic relationships is essential for protecting your self-esteem and emotional well-being. Recognize the signs of toxicity, understand their impact on your self-esteem, and take proactive steps to deal with toxic relationships effectively. By setting boundaries, prioritizing self-care, seeking resolution when possible, detaching when necessary, and surrounding yourself with supportive relationships, you can create a healthier and more positive environment that fosters

Cultivating a support network of positive and empowering individuals

Cultivating a support network is essential for our emotional well-being, personal growth, and resilience. A support network consists of individuals who provide us with encouragement, understanding, and assistance during both good times and challenging moments. These individuals form a safety net that helps us navigate life's ups and downs and provides a sense of belonging and connection.

A support network can be made up of various types of relationships, including family members, close friends, mentors, colleagues, or members of a community or support group. What matters most is that these individuals are reliable, trustworthy, and genuinely care about our well-being. They offer a listening ear, a shoulder to lean on, and a non-judgmental space where we can freely express ourselves.

Cultivating a support network involves both building and nurturing relationships. It starts by actively seeking out connections with people who share our values, interests, or goals. Engaging in activities, joining social or community groups, or participating in hobbies or volunteering can help us meet like-minded individuals who may become part of our support network.

Nurturing a support network requires on-going effort and investment. It involves being present for others, offering support, and actively engaging in reciprocal relationships. It means being a good listener, showing empathy, and providing encouragement and assistance when needed. Building trust and open communication are vital components of cultivating a strong support network.

A support network offers numerous benefits. It provides emotional support during difficult times, offering comfort and understanding when we face challenges or setbacks. It provides a sense of validation and affirmation, reminding us that we are not alone in our experiences. A support network can also offer different perspectives, advice, and guidance that can broaden our understanding and help us make informed decisions.

Moreover, a support network contributes to personal growth and resilience. By surrounding ourselves with supportive individuals, we gain confidence, expand our knowledge and skills, and are more likely to pursue our goals and dreams. They provide motivation, accountability, and inspiration to help us overcome obstacles and persevere.

In summary, cultivating a support network is crucial for our well-being and personal growth. By intentionally building and nurturing connections with individuals who offer support, understanding, and encouragement, we create a foundation for emotional strength and resilience. A support network provides us with the resources and connections we need to thrive and navigate life's challenges with greater confidence and ease.

Building a support network of positive and empowering individuals is crucial for our personal growth, well-being, and overall success. These individuals can provide encouragement, guidance, and inspiration during both the highs and lows of life.

1. The Importance of a Support Network: A support network is a group of individuals who uplift, motivate, and support us. They offer emotional support, provide different perspectives, and celebrate our achievements. A strong support network boosts our self-esteem, provides a sense of belonging, and helps us navigate challenges with resilience.

2. Assessing Your Current Network: Evaluate your current relationships and determine which ones are positive and empowering. Identify individuals who genuinely care about your well-being, share your values, and support your goals and aspirations. Recognize those who bring positivity, encouragement, and inspiration into your life.

3. Expanding Your Social Circle: To cultivate a support network, seek opportunities to expand your social circle. Engage in activities and join communities or groups where you can meet like-minded individuals. Attend networking events, seminars, or workshops related to your interests and passions. Be open to connecting with new people and building meaningful relationships.

4. Building Trust and Authentic Connections: Nurture trust and authenticity in your relationships. Be open, vulnerable, and genuine in your interactions. Share your thoughts, aspirations, and challenges with those you trust. Encourage open and honest communication, and create a safe space where everyone feels comfortable sharing their experiences.

5. Nurturing Reciprocity: Foster reciprocity within your support network. Offer your support, encouragement, and assistance to others in their endeavors. Celebrate their achievements, provide a listening ear when needed, and be there for them in times of difficulty. Nurturing reciprocity creates a mutually beneficial and empowering environment.

6. Seeking Mentors and Role Models: Identify mentors and role models who inspire you and align with your goals. Seek their guidance, learn from their experiences, and observe how they navigate challenges. Engage in conversations with them, ask for advice, and seek opportunities to learn and grow under their mentorship.

7. Utilizing Online Platforms and Communities: Take advantage of online platforms and communities to connect with positive and empowering individuals. Join social media groups, forums, or online communities centered around your interests or personal development. Engage in meaningful conversations, share your experiences, and seek advice from like-minded individuals.
8. Creating Supportive Rituals and Activities: Establish supportive rituals and activities within your network. Organize regular meet-ups, gatherings, or virtual sessions where you can connect, share experiences, and support each other. Engage in activities such as book clubs, mastermind groups, or accountability partnerships to foster growth and empower each other.
9. Communicating Your Needs: Clearly communicate your needs within your support network. Let others know how they can best support you, whether it's through encouragement, constructive feedback, or simply being a listening ear. Be open about your goals, aspirations, and challenges, allowing others to provide the support you require.
10. Expressing Gratitude: Express gratitude for the individuals in your support network. Regularly acknowledge and appreciate their presence, contributions, and support. Show gratitude for their impact on your life, as it strengthens the bonds within your network and fosters a positive and empowering environment.

Cultivating a support network of positive and empowering individuals is a valuable investment in your personal growth and well-being. Assess your current relationships, expand your social circle, nurture authenticity and reciprocity, seek mentors and role models, utilize online platforms, create supportive rituals, and communicate

Techniques for fostering healthy relationships that uplifts and inspire

Fostering healthy relationships is vital for our overall well-being and happiness. Healthy relationships contribute to our personal growth, provide support during challenging times, and enhance our overall quality of life. Whether they are friendships, romantic partnerships, family relationships, or professional connections, healthy relationships share common characteristics that promote mutual respect, trust, and emotional well-being.

Fostering healthy relationships that uplift and inspire us is essential for our overall well-being, personal growth, and happiness. These relationships provide a supportive foundation, encourage us to reach our full potential, and bring joy into our lives. Building and nurturing healthy relationships require intentional effort and certain principles. Here are some key aspects to consider:

1. Communication: Effective communication is the foundation of a healthy relationship. It involves active listening, expressing oneself honestly and respectfully, and being open to understanding the other person's perspective. Clear and open communication fosters understanding, resolves conflicts, and strengthens the bond between individuals.
2. Trust and Honesty: Trust is essential for any healthy relationship. Building trust involves being reliable, keeping promises, and being honest with one another. Trust creates a sense of safety, emotional security, and allows for vulnerability and deepening connections.
3. Respect and Boundaries: Respecting each other's boundaries, opinions, and autonomy is crucial in maintaining a healthy relationship. It involves honoring each other's needs, values, and personal space. Establishing and respecting boundaries ensures that

both individuals feel safe, valued, and heard within the relationship.

4. Empathy and Understanding: Practicing empathy involves putting oneself in the other person's shoes, understanding their feelings, and showing compassion. It is about being sensitive to their experiences and validating their emotions. Empathy builds connection, fosters understanding, and strengthens emotional intimacy.
5. Support and Encouragement: Healthy relationships involve providing support, encouragement, and celebrating each other's successes. Being there for one another during difficult times and offering a helping hand promotes a sense of security, builds trust, and strengthens the bond between individuals.
6. Conflict Resolution: Conflict is a natural part of any relationship, but healthy relationships involve resolving conflicts constructively. It requires effective communication, active listening, and a willingness to find mutually beneficial solutions. Seeking resolution through compromise and understanding helps maintain a harmonious and healthy relationship.
7. Quality Time and Shared Activities: Spending quality time together and engaging in shared activities strengthens the bond between individuals. It creates opportunities for connection, deepens understanding, and builds shared memories. Making time for each other demonstrates the importance of the relationship.
8. Individual Growth and Support: Healthy relationships support each other's personal growth and aspirations. Encouraging individual goals, providing support, and celebrating achievements contribute to the overall well-being of both individuals and the relationship itself.
9. Practice Effective Communication: Effective communication is the cornerstone of healthy

relationships. Listen actively, seeking to understand rather than simply respond. Express yourself honestly, assertively, and respectfully. Communicate your needs, boundaries, and emotions openly, fostering a climate of trust, understanding, and mutual respect.

10. Show Empathy and Understanding: Empathy plays a vital role in fostering healthy relationships. Seek to understand others' perspectives, emotions, and experiences. Practice active empathy by putting yourself in their shoes and showing genuine care and compassion. Validate their feelings and experiences, creating an atmosphere of understanding and support.
11. Nurture Positivity and Gratitude: Cultivate positivity and gratitude within your relationships. Express appreciation for the people in your life, acknowledging their contributions and qualities. Focus on the positive aspects of your interactions and celebrate each other's successes. Embrace a positive Mind-set and cultivate an uplifting atmosphere.
12. Support Each Other's Growth: Encourage and support each other's personal growth and aspirations. Celebrate achievements and milestones, offering sincere praise and encouragement. Provide constructive feedback when necessary, with kindness and respect. Actively listen to each other's goals, dreams, and challenges, offering guidance and assistance along the way.
13. Respect Boundaries and Autonomy: Respect each other's boundaries and individual autonomy. Recognize that everyone has different needs, preferences, and limits. Honor those boundaries, refraining from imposing your own expectations or judgments. Create a space where each person feels safe and empowered to be their authentic self.
14. Foster Trust and Reliability: Build trust within your relationships through consistent and reliable behavior.

Be trustworthy and dependable, following through on your commitments and promises. Maintain confidentiality and demonstrate integrity in your actions. Trust forms the foundation for healthy and meaningful connections.

15. Practice Active Listening: Develop the skill of active listening to foster deeper connections. Give your full attention to the person speaking, without interrupting or judging. Seek to understand their thoughts, feelings, and experiences. Ask clarifying questions and reflect back their words to show that you are truly present and engaged.

16. Celebrate Individuality and Uniqueness: Embrace and celebrate each other's individuality and uniqueness. Recognize that diversity and differences enrich relationships. Appreciate and respect the strengths, talents, and perspectives that each person brings to the table. Encourage authenticity and create an environment where everyone feels valued and accepted.

17. Resolve Conflict Constructively: Conflict is inevitable in any relationship. Learn constructive conflict resolution techniques, such as active listening, expressing emotions without blame, and finding win-win solutions. Approach conflicts with an open mind and a willingness to understand and find common ground. Use conflicts as opportunities for growth and deeper connection.

18. Practice Forgiveness and Letting Go: Forgiveness is essential for maintaining healthy relationships. Learn to forgive and let go of past hurts and resentments. Holding onto grudges only hinders the growth and harmony within relationships. Practice forgiveness, both towards others and yourself, promoting healing, understanding, and stronger bonds.

Cultivating healthy relationships that uplift and inspire us requires effort, patience, and empathy. By practicing effective communication, showing empathy, nurturing positivity and gratitude, supporting each other's growth, respecting boundaries, fostering trust, practicing active listening, celebrating individuality, resolving conflicts constructively, and practicing forgiveness, we can create relationships that bring joy.

By fostering healthy relationships based on these principles, we create a supportive and nurturing environment that enriches our lives and promotes personal happiness and fulfillment. Remember that building healthy relationships takes time, effort, and continuous commitment from all individuals involved.

10

Success and Failure: Embracing the Journey

Success and failure are integral parts of our personal and professional journeys. They shape our experiences, teach us valuable lessons, and contribute to our growth. The journey to success and failure is a fundamental part of life. It is a dynamic process that involves both achievements and setbacks, growth and learning, and the exploration of our capabilities and limitations. Understanding and embracing this journey can provide valuable insights, resilience, and personal development.

The path to success is often paved with hard work, determination, and perseverance. It requires setting goals, creating a vision, and taking consistent action towards realizing our aspirations. Along the way, we may encounter obstacles, face failures, and experience setbacks. However, these challenges offer valuable opportunities for growth, learning, and self-discovery.

Failure, contrary to its negative connotation, is an integral part of the journey to success. It teaches us valuable lessons, helps us understand our strengths and weaknesses, and provides opportunities for course correction and improvement. Failure is not the end, but rather a stepping stone towards growth and success. Embracing failure as a learning experience allows us to refine our strategies, develop resilience, and deepen our self-awareness.

The journey to success and failure is unique to each individual. It is a deeply personal and subjective experience, influenced by our aspirations, values, and definition of success. It is essential to define success on our own terms rather than being solely guided by societal standards or external expectations.

Along the journey, it is crucial to maintain a positive mind-set, celebrate small victories, and practice self-compassion. Acknowledging and appreciating progress, no matter how small, keeps us motivated and engaged. It is equally important to cultivate a support network of individuals who believe in our potential, provide encouragement, and offer guidance during challenging times.

Success and failure are not binary outcomes but rather fluid and evolving concepts. They can coexist, and the journey to success is often a nonlinear process. It requires adaptability, flexibility, and the willingness to take risks. It is through embracing both success and failure that we can gain a deeper understanding of ourselves, develop resilience, and find fulfillment in our pursuits.

Remember, the journey to success and failure is not solely about the destination but the growth, learning, and transformation that occur along the way. Embrace the challenges, celebrate the victories, and continue moving forward with courage and determination. It is through this journey that we discover our true potential and create a meaningful and fulfilling life.

1. Redefining Success and Failure: Redefine your perspective on success and failure. Rather than viewing success solely as the achievement of specific outcomes and failure as a negative outcome, consider them as part of a continuous learning process. Success can be seen as progress, growth, and the fulfillment of personal goals, while failure becomes an opportunity for growth, resilience, and course correction.

2. Embracing Failure as a Learning Experience: Shift your Mind-set and embrace failure as a valuable learning

experience. Recognize that failure is not a reflection of your worth, but a natural part of the journey toward success. Analyze the lessons learned from failure, identify areas for improvement, and adjust your approach accordingly. Embracing failure allows for personal and professional growth.

3. Cultivating Resilience: Resilience is the ability to bounce back from setbacks and adversity. Cultivate resilience by developing a growth Mind-set, which focuses on learning and improvement rather than fixed abilities. Embrace challenges, view them as opportunities for growth, and maintain a positive attitude in the face of obstacles. Resilience allows you to persevere and continue moving forward.
4. Setting Realistic Expectations: Set realistic expectations for yourself and your journey. Understand that success does not happen overnight and that failure is a natural part of the process. Avoid comparing your progress to others and focus on your own growth and development. Set meaningful goals that align with your values and passions, allowing for continuous improvement and a sense of fulfillment.
5. Practicing Self-Reflection: Engage in regular self-reflection to gain insight into your experiences, successes, and failures. Reflect on your strengths, weaknesses, and areas for growth. Identify patterns and behaviors that contribute to your success or hinder your progress. Self-reflection helps you make informed decisions, learn from your experiences, and make adjustments along the way.
6. Celebrating Success: Celebrate your successes, no matter how small they may seem. Acknowledge your achievements, milestones, and personal growth. Celebrating success boosts your confidence, reinforces positive behavior, and provides motivation to keep

striving for more. Take time to appreciate your accomplishments and the effort you put into reaching your goals.

7. Finding Inspiration in Others: Seek inspiration from individuals who have experienced both success and failure. Learn from their journeys, their perseverance, and their ability to overcome challenges. Surround yourself with mentors, role models, or a supportive community that shares their experiences and insights. Drawing inspiration from others can fuel your own motivation and determination.

8. Maintaining a Growth Mind-set: Maintain a growth Mind-set throughout your journey. Embrace challenges as opportunities for growth, view setbacks as temporary, and believe in your ability to learn and improve. Emphasize the process rather than the outcome, recognizing that true success lies in continuous growth and development.

9. Seeking Support and Feedback: Seek support and feedback from trusted individuals who can provide guidance and perspective. Surround yourself with a supportive network that believes in your potential and encourages your growth. Welcome constructive criticism as an opportunity for improvement, and be open to receiving feedback to enhance your skills and knowledge.

10. Finding Joy in the Journey: Above all, find joy in the journey itself. Embrace the ups and downs, the successes and failures, as they contribute to your growth and personal fulfillment. Enjoy the process of learning, exploring, and overcoming challenges. By finding joy in the journey, you can maintain a sense of fulfillment and gratitude, regardless of the specific outcomes. Remember that success and failure are not endpoints but rather markers along the path of personal and professional growth.

Embracing the journey of success and failure is essential for personal fulfillment and growth. By redefining success and failure, embracing failure as a learning experience, cultivating resilience, setting realistic expectations, practicing self-reflection, celebrating success, finding inspiration in others, maintaining a growth Mind-set, seeking support and feedback, and finding joy in the journey, you can navigate the ups and downs with confidence and resilience. Remember that success and failure are not isolated events but interconnected elements of a continuous journey toward personal and professional fulfillment. Embrace both the successes and failures, learn from them, and keep moving forward on your path to personal growth and happiness.

Rethinking Success and Failure as Opportunities for Growth

Rethinking success and failure involves challenging traditional notions and reframing our perspectives on these concepts. It is an invitation to question societal expectations, redefine our personal definitions, and explore alternative ways of measuring achievement and growth.

In conventional terms, success is often associated with external markers such as wealth, status, or recognition. However, true success is subjective and deeply personal. It can be found in the pursuit of meaningful goals, the cultivation of fulfilling relationships, the development of personal well-being, or the contribution to a greater cause.

Rethinking success encourages us to align our goals and aspirations with our core values, passions, and purpose. It invites us to consider the impact we want to make on our own lives and the lives of others. By focusing on personal fulfillment and a sense of purpose, we can redefine success in ways that are authentic and meaningful to us.

Similarly, rethinking failure involves shifting our perspective from a negative and discouraging experience to a valuable learning opportunity. Failure is not a reflection of our worth or abilities but rather a natural part of the learning process. It offers valuable insights, highlights areas for growth, and builds resilience.

By reframing failure as a stepping stone on the path to success, we can embrace it with curiosity and a growth mindset. Each failure becomes an opportunity for self-reflection, adjustment, and improvement. It teaches us resilience, persistence, and the importance of adapting our strategies.

Rethinking success and failure encourages us to detach our self-worth from external achievements and instead focus on personal growth, well-being, and the pursuit of our passions. It invites us to celebrate progress, acknowledge small victories, and practice self-compassion throughout the journey.

Ultimately, rethinking success and failure empowers us to define our own paths, set our own goals, and measure our progress based on our unique values and aspirations. It liberates us from societal pressures, fosters a sense of authenticity, and allows us to create a life that aligns with our true selves.

As you embark on the journey of rethinking success and failure, remember that it is a deeply personal exploration. Take the time to reflect on what truly matters to you, challenge societal norms, and embrace a perspective that resonates with your values and aspirations. In doing so, you can redefine success and failure in ways that bring you greater fulfillment, purpose, and joy.

Our perception of success and failure has a significant impact on our personal growth and development. By redefining these concepts and viewing them as opportunities for growth, we can cultivate a Mind-set that embraces challenges, learns from setbacks, and maximizes our potential.

Success and failure both play significant roles as opportunities for growth and personal development. They offer different perspectives and experiences that contribute to our learning, resilience, and overall growth as individuals. Here's a closer look at the roles of success and failure in our journey of growth:

1. Success as a Catalyst for Growth: Successes provide moments of accomplishment and validation for our efforts. They reinforce our skills, abilities, and strategies, boosting our confidence and motivation. Successes can serve as a launching pad for further growth, pushing us to set higher goals and strive for even more significant achievements. They validate our capabilities, provide a sense of progress, and inspire us to continue expanding our boundaries.

2. Failure as a Teacher: Failure, on the other hand, is a powerful teacher that offers valuable lessons and insights. It highlights areas where we can improve, exposes weaknesses or gaps in our knowledge, and presents opportunities for self-reflection and course correction. Failure teaches us resilience, determination, and adaptability. It helps us develop problem-solving skills, learn from mistakes, and gain a deeper understanding of ourselves and our capabilities.

3. Learning from Mistakes: Failure encourages us to analyze what went wrong and learn from our mistakes. It prompts us to identify alternative approaches, develop new strategies, and make necessary adjustments. Each failure brings us closer to success by providing feedback and guidance on areas that need improvement. It teaches us to view setbacks as stepping stones rather than permanent roadblocks.

4. Embracing Growth Mind-set: Both success and failure contribute to the development of a growth mind-set. A growth mind-set is the belief that abilities and intelligence can be developed through dedication, effort, and learning. It enables us to see challenges as

opportunities for growth, embrace failures as learning experiences, and persist in the face of setbacks. With a growth mind-set, we view success and failure as part of a continuous learning process, fostering resilience and a willingness to take on new challenges.

5. Building Resilience: Success and failure both build resilience, albeit in different ways. Successes enhance our belief in our abilities and provide us with the confidence to tackle future challenges. They reinforce our resilience by showing us that we have the capacity to overcome obstacles and achieve our goals. On the other hand, failure builds resilience by teaching us to bounce back from setbacks, persevere in the face of adversity, and maintain a positive outlook despite temporary failures.
6. Holistic Growth and Balance: The interplay between success and failure contributes to holistic growth. It teaches us the importance of balance and recognizing that growth is not solely defined by achievements but also by personal well-being, relationships, and fulfillment in various aspects of life. Both success and failure guide us toward a more comprehensive understanding of ourselves, our values, and our goals, leading to a more well-rounded and fulfilling journey of growth.
7. Redefining Success: Instead of defining success solely by external achievements or societal expectations, redefine it based on your own values, passions, and personal growth. Consider success as the continuous pursuit of self-improvement, the fulfillment of your potential, and the alignment of your actions with your values. Focus on progress, learning, and meaningful experiences rather than solely on specific outcomes.
8. Embracing a Growth Mind-set: Adopt a growth Mind-set, which views challenges and setbacks as

opportunities for learning and growth. Embrace the belief that your abilities and intelligence can be developed through dedication and effort. See failures and mistakes as stepping stones toward improvement, and approach them with curiosity and a willingness to learn from them.

9. Shifting Perspective on Failure: Reframe failure as feedback and a necessary part of the learning process. Understand that failure does not define your worth or potential. Instead, view it as an opportunity to gain valuable insights, identify areas for improvement, and adjust your approach. Embrace the lessons learned from failures and use them as fuel for personal growth.

10. Embracing a Growth-Oriented Goal Setting: Set growth-oriented goals that focus on personal development, learning, and progress rather than solely on specific outcomes. Break down your goals into smaller, achievable steps that allow for continuous improvement. Celebrate each milestone reached and use setbacks as opportunities to reflect, adjust, and refine your approach.

11. Cultivating a Learning Mind-set: Cultivate a Mind-set of continuous learning and self-improvement. Seek out new knowledge, skills, and experiences. Embrace challenges that push you out of your comfort zone and provide opportunities for growth. Engage in self-reflection, seeking feedback, and actively seeking opportunities to expand your knowledge and skills.

12. Practicing Self-Compassion: Practice self-compassion when facing setbacks or challenges. Treat yourself with kindness and understanding, recognizing that setbacks are a natural part of the growth process. Acknowledge your efforts, progress, and strengths, and learn from your mistakes with a gentle and supportive attitude toward yourself.

13. Surrounding Yourself with Supportive Individuals: Surround yourself with supportive individuals who encourage your growth and provide constructive feedback. Seek mentors, coaches, or like-minded individuals who inspire and challenge you to reach your full potential. Engage in communities or networks that foster a growth-oriented Mind-set and provide a supportive environment for learning and development.
14. Reflecting and Evaluating: Regularly reflect on your experiences, successes, and failures. Evaluate your progress and identify areas for growth and improvement. Embrace a Mind-set of continuous self-assessment and use your reflections as a guide for future actions. Celebrate your successes and acknowledge the lessons learned from failures to inform your future endeavors.
15. Embracing Resilience and Persistence: Develop resilience and persistence as key traits in your personal growth journey. Embrace challenges, setbacks, and obstacles as opportunities to build resilience and develop problem-solving skills. Cultivate the determination to persevere, even in the face of difficulties, and use setbacks as motivation to keep moving forward.

By rethinking success and failure as opportunities for growth, we can transform our Mind-set and approach to personal and professional development. In summary, success and failure serve as complementary elements in our growth journey. They provide opportunities for learning, self-reflection, and personal development. By embracing both success and failure, we can cultivate resilience, expand our capabilities, and continuously evolve on our path toward becoming our best selves.

Developing a Healthy Relationship with Achievement

Achievement is often valued and pursued in various aspects of life, but developing a healthy relationship with it is essential for our well-being and long-term satisfaction. By cultivating a balanced perspective and adopting healthy attitudes toward achievement, we can experience fulfillment and maintain a positive Mind-set.

Developing a healthy relationship with achievement is an important aspect of personal growth and fulfillment. Achievement, in its various forms, can bring a sense of accomplishment, recognition, and success. However, it is equally important to cultivate a balanced and healthy perspective towards achievement, ensuring that it contributes to our overall well-being and happiness.

In our society, there is often an emphasis on external markers of achievement, such as academic or professional success, financial wealth, or social recognition. While these achievements can be meaningful, it is crucial to remember that they are not the sole determinants of our self-worth or happiness. Developing a healthy relationship with achievement involves a shift in mind-set and a focus on holistic well-being.

A healthy relationship with achievement involves several key elements:

1. Defining Personal Values: To develop a healthy relationship with achievement, it is essential to align our goals and pursuits with our personal values. Reflecting on what truly matters to us and setting goals that are in line with our values ensures that our achievements are meaningful and fulfilling. It allows us to pursue goals that bring genuine satisfaction and contribute to our overall well-being.
2. Embracing the Journey: Developing a healthy relationship with achievement means placing

importance on the journey rather than solely focusing on the end result. Recognizing that growth, learning, and self-discovery occur throughout the process encourages us to appreciate the progress made, regardless of the outcome. Embracing the journey allows us to derive fulfillment from the experiences, lessons learned, and personal development that occur along the way.

3. Celebrating Small Victories: While major achievements are worth acknowledging, it is equally important to celebrate the small victories along the path. Recognizing and appreciating the smaller milestones and accomplishments helps to build motivation, boost self-confidence, and maintain a positive outlook. Celebrating these moments of progress reinforces a healthy relationship with achievement by shifting the focus from the final destination to the joy of continuous growth and improvement.
4. Cultivating Balance and Well-being: A healthy relationship with achievement involves maintaining a sense of balance and prioritizing well-being. It means recognizing that success in one area of life should not come at the expense of other important aspects, such as relationships, self-care, and personal fulfillment. Striving for a well-rounded life and nurturing all areas of our well-being ensures that achievement is part of a holistic and fulfilling lifestyle.
5. Gratitude and Appreciation: Cultivating gratitude and appreciation for our achievements and the opportunities that have contributed to them is crucial. Recognizing the contributions of others, acknowledging our own efforts and strengths, and expressing gratitude for the journey and the lessons learned fosters a healthy and positive relationship with achievement. It helps to cultivate a mind-set of abundance, contentment, and fulfillment.

6. Define Success on Your Own Terms: Take the time to define what success means to you personally, rather than relying solely on external standards or societal expectations. Reflect on your values, passions, and aspirations to establish your own criteria for achievement. Align your goals and actions with what truly matters to you.

7. Embrace a Growth Mind-set: Adopt a growth Mind-set that emphasizes learning, development, and continuous improvement rather than a fixed Mind-set focused solely on outcomes. Embrace challenges as opportunities for growth and view setbacks as temporary obstacles on the path to success. Cultivate a belief in your ability to learn and develop new skills.

8. Celebrate Small Wins:Acknowledge and celebrate the smaller milestones and achievements along the way. Recognize that progress is a series of small steps and that each step is worth celebrating. By appreciating the smaller wins, you can maintain motivation and momentum on your journey toward larger goals.

9. Balance Ambition and Well-Being: Strive for a balance between ambition and well-being. Recognize that success does not come at the expense of your physical or mental health. Prioritize self-care, set boundaries, and maintain a healthy work-life balance. Remember that achieving goals is important, but taking care of yourself is equally vital for long-term happiness.

10. Focus on Intrinsic Motivation: Cultivate intrinsic motivation by finding joy and satisfaction in the process of pursuing your goals, rather than relying solely on external rewards or validation. Identify the intrinsic values and meaning behind your pursuits, and derive fulfillment from the journey itself. This shift in focus can enhance your sense of fulfillment and reduce the reliance on external factors.

11. Practice Gratitude and Contentment: Cultivate gratitude and contentment in your achievements. Instead of constantly chasing the next goal, take the time

Conclusion: Unleashing Your Inner Power

Throughout this guide, we have explored various aspects of personal growth, self-improvement, and developing a positive Mind-set. By implementing the strategies and techniques discussed, you can unleash your inner power and tap into your full potential. Here are some key takeaways to remember:

1. Self-Awareness: Start by developing self-awareness, understanding your strengths, weaknesses, values, and passions. This self-awareness forms the foundation for personal growth and empowers you to make conscious choices aligned with your true self.

2. Goal Setting: Set meaningful goals that align with your values and aspirations. Break them down into actionable steps and continuously monitor your progress. Remember to celebrate both small and significant milestones along the way.

3. Positive Mind-set: Cultivate a positive Mind-set by practicing gratitude, embracing optimism, and reframing challenges as opportunities for growth. Train your mind to focus on solutions and possibilities rather than dwelling on limitations.

4. Self-Care and Well-being: Prioritize self-care and well-being to maintain balance and resilience. Nourish your body with healthy habits, engage in activities that bring you joy, and prioritize rest and relaxation. Take care of your mental, emotional, and physical well-being.

5. Embracing Failure and Learning: Embrace failures and setbacks as valuable learning experiences. See them as stepping stones toward personal growth and use them to refine your approach. Adopt a growth Mind-set and see every challenge as an opportunity for improvement.
6. Building Supportive Relationships: Surround yourself with supportive individuals who uplift and inspire you. Cultivate a network of positive relationships that encourage your personal growth and provide a sense of belonging. Seek mentors and role models who can guide and inspire you on your journey.
7. Continuous Learning: Commit to lifelong learning and personal development. Seek opportunities for growth, whether through formal education, self-study, or new experiences. Stay curious and open-minded, always seeking new knowledge and insights.
8. Embracing Change and Adaptability: Embrace change as a constant in life and develop your adaptability skills. Be open to new perspectives, ideas, and opportunities. See change as an opportunity for personal growth and adaptation.
9. Taking Action: Ultimately, unleashing your inner power requires taking consistent action towards your goals and dreams. Break free from procrastination and take decisive steps towards your aspirations. Be resilient and persevere, even in the face of challenges and setbacks.

Remember, personal growth is a lifelong journey. It requires patience, self-compassion, and a commitment to continuous improvement. As you embrace your inner power, you will discover the strength, resilience, and potential that lies within you. Embrace the process, believe in yourself, and unleash your inner power to create a fulfilling and purposeful life.

Reflecting on the journey of building confidence, belief, and self-esteem

Unleashing your inner power is about tapping into your true potential, embracing your strengths, and overcoming self-limiting beliefs. It involves recognizing and honoring your unique qualities, passions, and values, and aligning them with your actions and goals. Here are a few key points to consider: Reflecting on the journey of building confidence, belief, and self-esteem allows us to appreciate the progress we have made and the lessons we have learned. It is a time to acknowledge the challenges we have overcome, the growth we have experienced, and the transformations that have taken place within us. Here are some points to consider during this reflection:

1. Self-Awareness: Develop a deep understanding of yourself - your values, beliefs, strengths, and weaknesses. This awareness allows you to leverage your strengths and work on areas that need improvement.

2. Belief in Yourself: Cultivate a strong belief in your abilities and potential. Challenge self-doubt and replace negative thoughts with positive affirmations. Embrace a growth mind-set and view failures as learning opportunities.

3. Confidence: Build confidence by stepping out of your comfort zone and taking on new challenges. Celebrate your achievements, no matter how small, and recognize your progress along the way.

4. Self-Care: Prioritize self-care and well-being. Nurture your physical, mental, and emotional health through activities like exercise, mindfulness, and healthy relationships.

5. Goal Setting: Set clear, achievable goals that align with your passions and values. Break them down into actionable steps and track your progress. Celebrate milestones and stay motivated.

6. Resilience: Embrace setbacks and failures as part of the journey. Develop resilience by bouncing back from challenges, adapting to change, and maintaining a positive outlook.

7. Surround Yourself with Support: Seek out positive and supportive relationships. Surround yourself with people who believe in you, provide encouragement, and inspire your growth.

8. Continuous Learning: Stay curious and committed to personal growth. Engage in lifelong learning, seek new experiences, and expand your knowledge and skills.

9. Authenticity: Embrace your uniqueness and let your true self shine. Be true to your values, passions, and purpose, and avoid comparing yourself to others.

10. Take Action: Unleash your inner power by taking consistent action towards your goals. Break through self-imposed limitations and step into your potential.

11. Awareness of Personal Growth: Take a moment to recognize how far you have come on your journey. Reflect on the areas where you have seen significant growth in your confidence, belief, and self-esteem. Consider the challenges you faced and the steps you took to overcome them. Celebrate the progress you have made and the positive changes you have witnessed in yourself.

12. Lessons Learned: Reflect on the lessons you have learned throughout this process. What insights have you gained about yourself, your capabilities, and your values? Consider the strategies and techniques that have

been most effective in building your confidence, belief, and self-esteem. Identify the patterns and habits that have hindered your progress, and use this knowledge to continue refining your approach.

13. Celebrating Achievements: Take the time to celebrate your achievements, both big and small. Acknowledge the milestones you have reached and the goals you have accomplished. Recognize the courage it took to step outside your comfort zone and the resilience you demonstrated in the face of challenges. Celebrate these achievements as evidence of your growth and as a source of motivation to keep striving for even greater things.
14. Gratitude and Self-Appreciation: Express gratitude for the people, experiences, and resources that have supported you on your journey. Acknowledge the support and encouragement you have received from loved ones, mentors, or coaches. Also, practice self-appreciation by recognizing and acknowledging your own efforts, strengths, and progress. Give yourself credit for the hard work and dedication you have invested in building your confidence, belief, and self-esteem.
15. Identifying Areas for Further Growth: Reflect on areas where you still have room for growth. Recognize that personal development is a continuous process and that there will always be new challenges and opportunities to explore. Identify specific areas where you would like to further enhance your confidence, belief, or self-esteem, and set new goals to continue your growth.
16. Maintaining Momentum: Reflect on how you can maintain the momentum of your personal growth journey. Consider the strategies, routines, or practices that have been most beneficial in sustaining your progress. Think about how you can continue to nurture

and cultivate your confidence, belief, and self-esteem on an ongoing basis. Create a plan to incorporate these practices into your daily life to ensure continued growth and self-improvement.

Remember, reflection is a powerful tool for personal growth and self-awareness. By taking the time to reflect on your journey of building confidence, belief, and self-esteem,

to appreciate and savor what you have accomplished. Express gratitude for the opportunities, resources, and support that have contributed to your achievements. Find contentment in the present moment while maintaining a sense of ambition for the future.

12. Embrace Failure as a Learning Opportunity: View failure as an inherent part of the achievement process rather than a reflection of your worth or abilities. Embrace failures as valuable learning experiences that provide insight and growth. Analyze what went wrong, extract lessons, and adjust your approach accordingly. Resilience in the face of failure is a key attribute in developing a healthy relationship with achievement.

13. Cultivate Self-Reflection: Regularly engage in self-reflection to evaluate your relationship with achievement. Assess whether your goals and pursuits align with your values and bring genuine fulfillment. Examine the impact of achievement on other areas of your life, such as relationships and well-being. Adjust your approach as needed to ensure harmony and balance.

14. Support and Collaborate with Others: Recognize that achievement is not a solitary endeavor. Seek support from and collaborate with others who share your values and goals. Surround yourself with a network of individuals who uplift and inspire you. Celebrate the achievements of others and offer support and encouragement in their pursuits.

Developing a healthy relationship with achievement involves aligning your goals with your values, embracing a growth Mind-set, celebrating small wins, balancing ambition and well-being, focusing on intrinsic motivation, practicing gratitude and contentment, embracing failure as a learning opportunity, engaging in self-reflection, and seeking support from others.

Developing a healthy relationship with achievement allows us to pursue goals and aspirations with a balanced perspective. It ensures that our pursuit of success is grounded in personal values, well-being, and a genuine sense of fulfillment. By embracing the journey, celebrating small victories, and maintaining a holistic perspective, we can navigate the realm of achievement in a way that enriches our lives and contributes to our overall well-being and happiness. you gain valuable insights, appreciate your progress, and set the stage for continued growth and success. Embrace this opportunity to celebrate your achievements, learn from your experiences, and continue your journey with renewed determination and purpose. Unleashing your inner power is a journey, not an overnight transformation. It requires patience, persistence, and a commitment to personal growth. By tapping into your inner strength, you can unleash your potential, achieve your goals, and live a fulfilled and purposeful life.

Final Words of Encouragement and Inspiration

As you embark on the journey of building confidence, belief, and self-esteem, I want to leave you with some final words of encouragement and inspiration:

1. You are capable of more than you realize: Believe in your potential and trust in your abilities. You have the power to overcome obstacles, achieve your goals, and create the life you desire. Have faith in yourself and never underestimate what you are capable of achieving.

2. Embrace the process: Building confidence, belief, and self-esteem is not an overnight transformation. It is a continuous process of growth and self-discovery. Embrace the ups and downs, the successes and setbacks, knowing that each experience contributes to your personal development.

3. Be kind to yourself: Remember to practice self-compassion along the way. Treat yourself with kindness, patience, and understanding. Acknowledge that everyone has their own unique journey, and it's okay to have moments of self-doubt. Be gentle with yourself and celebrate your progress, no matter how small.

4. Surround yourself with positivity: Surround yourself with people who uplift and inspire you. Seek out supportive relationships and communities that foster growth and positivity. Distance yourself from negativity and toxic influences that drain your energy and undermine your self-esteem.

5. Take courageous steps outside your comfort zone: Growth happens outside of your comfort zone. Challenge yourself to take small steps of bravery each day. Push through fear and embrace new experiences. Embrace the discomfort as a sign of personal growth and use it as fuel to propel you forward.

6. Practice gratitude: Cultivate an attitude of gratitude for the journey you are on. Appreciate the lessons, the opportunities, and the blessings that come your way. Gratitude opens your heart to abundance and helps you maintain a positive perspective.

7. Keep learning and evolving: Commit to a lifetime of learning and self-improvement. Seek knowledge, explore new interests, and continuously expand your

horizons. Embrace change and adaptability, as they are essential for personal growth and success.

8. Trust the process: Trust that the efforts you invest in building your confidence, belief, and self-esteem will yield results. Stay committed to your growth journey, even when progress seems slow or uncertain. Trust that each step you take is leading you closer to the confident and empowered person you aspire to be.

Remember, building confidence, belief, and self-esteem is a lifelong journey. It requires dedication, perseverance, and self-reflection. Be patient with yourself, stay focused on your goals, and never lose sight of the incredible potential that lies within you. Believe in yourself and your ability to create the life you deserve. You are capable, you are worthy, and you have the power to achieve greatness.

Guided Exercises for Building Confidence, Belief and Self-Esteem

Building confidence, belief, and self-esteem is an on-going process that requires practice and effort. Here are some exercises that can help strengthen these traits:

1. Positive Affirmations: Repeat positive affirmations to yourself daily. Affirmations are positive statements that reinforce your capabilities, strengths, and self-worth. Examples include "I am confident and capable," "I believe in myself and my abilities," and "I deserve success and happiness." Repeat these affirmations regularly to reprogram your subconscious mind and boost your self-belief.

2. Visualization: Visualize yourself succeeding and achieving your goals. Close your eyes and vividly imagine yourself confidently performing a task or reaching a desired outcome. Engage all your senses and focus on the positive emotions associated with your success. Visualization helps build belief in your abilities and creates a mental framework for success.

3. Celebrating Achievements: Acknowledge and celebrate your achievements, no matter how small. Take time to reflect on your accomplishments and give yourself credit for your efforts and progress. Celebrating your achievements reinforces a positive self-image and boosts your self-esteem.

4. Setting and Achieving Goals: Set realistic and achievable goals for yourself. Break them down into smaller, manageable steps and track your progress. As you achieve

these milestones, your confidence and belief in your abilities will grow. Each success fuels your self-esteem and motivates you to take on more challenging goals.

5. Facing Fears: Step out of your comfort zone and confront your fears. Identify an area where you feel limited by self-doubt or fear, and gradually expose yourself to that situation. Start with small steps and gradually increase the challenge. As you face your fears and overcome obstacles, your confidence and self-esteem will strengthen.

6. Practicing Self-Compassion: Treat yourself with kindness and compassion. Be mindful of your inner self-talk and replace negative self-criticism with supportive and understanding language. Practice self-care and prioritize your well-being. Cultivating self-compassion helps you build a positive self-image and fosters resilience in the face of setbacks.

7. Learning and Skill Development: Engage in continuous learning and skill development. Acquiring new knowledge and honing your skills enhances your competence and confidence. Seek opportunities for personal and professional growth, such as taking courses, attending workshops, or joining relevant communities.

8. Surrounding Yourself with Positive Influences: Surround yourself with positive and supportive individuals who believe in you and uplift your spirits. Seek out mentors, friends, or support groups that provide encouragement, feedback, and constructive guidance. Positive influences can boost your confidence, belief, and self-esteem.

9. Self-Reflection: Take time each day for self-reflection. Set aside a few minutes to sit quietly and think about your strengths, accomplishments, and the positive

qualities that define you. Reflect on moments when you felt confident and capable. Write them down in a journal to reinforce these positive aspects of yourself.

10. Affirmations: Create a list of positive affirmations that resonate with you. These are short, powerful statements that affirm your worth and capabilities. Repeat them daily, either silently or out loud, to reinforce positive beliefs about yourself. For example, say, "I am capable of achieving my goals," or "I believe in my abilities and talents."

11. Visualization: Close your eyes and visualize yourself successfully accomplishing a goal or facing a challenging situation with confidence. Imagine the details of the scene—the sights, sounds, and feelings of success. Visualization helps program your mind for success and boosts your belief in your abilities.

12. Step-by-Step Goal Setting: Break down your larger goals into smaller, achievable steps. Each step you accomplish reinforces your belief in your ability to achieve the bigger goal. Set realistic deadlines and track your progress along the way. Celebrate each milestone to boost your confidence.

13. Celebrating Achievements: Take time to acknowledge and celebrate your achievements, no matter how small they may seem. Write them down in a journal or share them with a supportive friend or family member. Celebrating your accomplishments reinforces your belief in your abilities and boosts your self-esteem.

14. Positive Self-Talk: Pay attention to your internal dialogue and replace negative self-talk with positive and empowering statements. When you catch yourself doubting or criticizing yourself, consciously reframe those thoughts into positive and supportive statements. For example, replace "I can't do this" with "I am capable of handling this challenge."

15. Facing Fears: Identify one fear or limiting belief that is holding you back. Break it down into smaller steps and gradually expose yourself to those steps. As you face your fears, you will prove to yourself that you are capable and resilient, which boosts your confidence and self-esteem.
16. Gratitude Practice: Develop a daily gratitude practice. Each day, write down three things you are grateful for. Focusing on the positive aspects of your life and cultivating gratitude shifts your perspective and helps you appreciate your own worth and the abundance around you.
17. Surround Yourself with Supportive People: Seek out relationships with people who believe in you, support your growth, and uplift you. Surrounding yourself with positive and encouraging individuals can greatly enhance your confidence, belief, and self-esteem.
18. Personal Growth Activities: Engage in activities that promote personal growth and self-discovery, such as reading self-help books, attending workshops or seminars, practicing mindfulness or meditation, or participating in therapy or coaching. These activities provide valuable insights and tools for building confidence, belief, and self-esteem.

Remember, building confidence, belief, and self-esteem is a continuous process. Consistency and practice are key. Be patient with yourself, stay committed to your personal growth, and practice these exercises consistently. With time and effort, you will witness a positive transformation in your confidence, belief, and self-esteem. Incorporate these guided exercises into your daily routine to cultivate a strong foundation of self-confidence and a positive self-image. With time and effort, you will experience significant growth and empowerment in various aspects of your life.